Entering Into the Heart of Jesus

Meditations on the Indwelling Trinity in St. John's Gospel

Entering Into the Heart of Jesus

Meditations on the Indwelling Trinity in St. John's Gospel

George A. Maloney, SJ

ALBA · HOUSE   NEW · YORK

SOCIETY OF ST. PAUL, 2187 VICTORY BLVD., STATEN ISLAND, NEW YORK 10314

Library of Congress Cataloging-in-Publication Data

Maloney, George A., 1924 -
  Entering into the heart of Jesus.

  1. Bible.   N.T.   John — Meditation.   2. Mystical
union — Meditations.   I.   Title.
BS2615.4.M35   1988   231'.044   87-30659
ISBN 0-8189-0527-1

Imprimi Potest:
Rev. Patrick Burns, S.J.
Provincial of Wisconsin Province
1987

_____

Designed, printed and bound in the United States of
America by the Fathers and Brothers of the
Society of St. Paul, 2187 Victory Boulevard,
Staten Island, New York 10314, as part of their
communications apostolate.

_____

  2 3 4 5 6 7 8 9 (Current Printing: first digit)

_____

DEDICATION

To
Joan Prime
who first suggested that I write a book
on the
spirituality found in St. John's Gospel

ACKNOWLEDGMENTS

Sincere gratitude to Mrs. Patricia Metta for typing the manuscript, and to Sister Joseph Agnes, S.C.H. and Mrs. June Culver for careful reading and correcting of the manuscript and for other suggestions that proved most helpful.

Thanks are due to the Bruce Publishing Company for permission to use its translation of the New Testament as the basic text of this book: *The New Testament*, Part One: *The Four Gospels*; translated by James A. Kleist, S.J. and Part Two: *Acts of the Apostles, Epistles and Apocalypse*; translated by Joseph L. Lilly, C.M. (Milwaukee, WI: The Bruce Publishing Company, 1956). I purposely chose this version because I found it to be a very exact translation from the Greek and one that still maintained an attractive English style of expression.

TABLE OF CONTENTS

ABBREVIATIONS

OLD TESTAMENT

Genesis	Gn	Proverbs	Pr
Exodus	Ex	Ecclesiastes	Ec
Leviticus	Lv	Song of Songs	Sg
Numbers	Nb	Wisdom	Ws
Deuteronomy	Dt	Sirach	Si
Joshua	Jos	Isaiah	Is
Judges	Jg	Jeremiah	Jr
Ruth	Rt	Lamentations	Lm
1 Samuel	1 S	Baruch	Ba
2 Samuel	2 S	Ezekiel	Ezk
1 Kings	1 K	Daniel	Dn
2 Kings	2 K	Hosea	Ho
1 Chronicles	1 Ch	Joel	Jl
2 Chronicles	2 Ch	Amos	Am
Ezra	Ezr	Obadiah	Ob
Nehemiah	Ne	Jonah	Jon
Tobit	Tb	Micah	Mi
Judith	Jdt	Nahum	Na
Esther	Est	Habakkuk	Hab
1 Maccabees	1 M	Zephaniah	Zp
2 Maccabees	2 M	Haggai	Hg
Job	Jb	Malachi	Ml
Psalms	Ps	Zechariah	Zc

NEW TESTAMENT

Matthew	Mt	1 Timothy	1 Tm
Mark	Mk	2 Timothy	2 Tm
Luke	Lk	Titus	Tt
John	Jn	Philemon	Phm
Acts	Ac	Hebrews	Heb
Romans	Rm	James	Jm
1 Corinthians	1 Cor	1 Peter	1 P
2 Corinthins	2 Cor	2 Peter	2 P
Galatians	Gal	1 John	1 Jn
Ephesians	Ep	2 John	2 Jn
Philippians	Ph	3 John	3 Jn
Colossians	Col	Jude	Jude
1 Thessalonians	1 Th	Revelation	Rv
2 Thessalonians	2 Th		

INTRODUCTION

THE GREAT REVELATION God has made to the human race is: "God is love" (1 Jn 4:8). Christianity maintains that Jesus Christ is God's perfect revelation. Jesus is the fulfiller of that revelation of God's love as active, immanently present to His children in *communion* through the self-emptying love unto the death of His only begotten Son. "So marked, indeed, has been God's love for the world that he gave his only begotten Son: everyone who believes in him is not to perish, but to have eternal life" (Jn 3:16-17).

Christianity, especially as developed in the West, has all too often accentuated the intellectual grasp of truths revealed by God through His Church and failed to see faith *in* Jesus Christ as a response we are to make to His gift of Himself to us. Understanding with our minds that God is love, as shown by Christ's dying on the cross for us, we have been exhorted by our teachers and preachers, therefore, to love others in the same sort of selfless way.

We have not heard enough of what the early Church Fathers — theologians who prayed out and experienced Scripture — continually taught of the inner transformation experienced in prayer through the regeneration of the Holy Spirit (Jn 3:3, 5). The middle stage between God's love for us and our going out in acts of service toward others has been slighted in our teaching and preaching.

We fear to preach another knowledge, one that is experiential, mystical and unifying of ourselves with God in a community of love — love, as Teilhard de Chardin describes, that differentiates as it unites. Jesus, as the perfect image of the Father's love for us, became human in order that by His death and resurrection and through His outpouring of the Holy Spirit, we all might come to "know" (Yada in Hebrew), by a person-to-person experience, that God loves us as a self-giving community of love.

EXPERIENCING GOD

IF GOD IS LOVE, this must mean — as Jesus has revealed it to us through Scripture which was handed down to us through the Church-Community of faith — that God, as community of Father, Son and Holy Spirit, wishes to give Himself to us. True love is expressed through the gift of self to the beloved. Jesus is God's gift of Himself to us through the Holy Spirit. We recognize this gift through faith. "The love of God has been poured into our hearts by the Holy Spirit which has been given us" (Rm 5:5). Through God's two hands, Jesus Christ and the Holy Spirit — as St. Irenaeus of the 2nd century expresses it in Johannine terms — we are touched by God.

If Jesus promised that He and the Father would come and dwell within us (Jn 14:23), why should we not experience that living presence? If Jesus taught that "eternal life is this: to know you, the only true God, and Jesus Christ whom you have sent" (Jn 17:3), why should it be so extraordinary to experience such knowledge: God loving us through the perfect gift of Himself as a triune community?

Whatever happened to Christ's chief revelation about the indwelling of the Trinity in the individual Christian and within the community of love we call the Body of Christ? Jesus came to bring us life. This is meant to be an ongoing process of knowing and loving God as the basic community of all loves, of experiencing profoundly the unique personhood of the Father, Son and Holy Spirit in their one divine nature.

Christianity was meant by Jesus to be a living experience of *abiding in* the Trinitarian community, loved infinitely by the Father in His Son, Jesus Christ, through His Holy Spirit. In earlier centuries of Christianity theology was the expression of a living, ongoing mystical experience of the indwelling Trinity. The central teaching of the Church revolved around the concept of *theosis*, the deification of the Christian through the work of the Holy Spirit released by the risen Jesus Christ. In this process one becomes a child of God (1 Jn 3:1) and an heir, with Christ, of heaven.

These theologians — and John the Evangelist was always considered *the* theologian and model for them all — were the seasoned ascetics who, pure in heart, were caught up in the non-objectified, mysterious, circular movement of triadic love. They were taught a knowledge of God that was not different from experienced love of God. And they taught, not by relaying to others a system of abstract truths about God, but by leading other Christians into the mystery of God.

But when speculative theology became divorced from the mysticism of John and Paul, the doctrine of the Trinity became something taught, to which Christians gave an intellectual assent and accepted as true. It was not taught and preached, though, as the most "practical" revealed truth of all, having transforming effects on our understanding of God, Christ, ourselves, the Church and the world.

Karl Rahner complains with great disappointment in his book, *The Trinity*, that, if this doctrine were to be declared unnecessary to the Christian faith, few Christian lives would be affected, and sadly enough, he writes, ". . . the major part of religious literature could well remain virtually unchanged."

THE WORLD
OF JOHN THE EVANGELIST

IT IS BECAUSE the Gospel of John is considered the most theological in the sense explained above and the most spiritual or
mystical (because it is here that we receive the revelation of
Jesus and the teaching of the early disciples on the indwelling
Trinity) that John in Christian art is pictured as an eagle. He has
a most penetrating gaze into the hidden mysteries of the very
community of triune love that explodes into creation in order
that the Trinity might share its very own life with us, made in
God's Logos.

Prayerfully reading this Gospel requires a knowledge
given by the Holy Spirit who "reaches the depths of everything,
even the depths of God" (1 Cor 2:11). This is the "hidden
wisdom of God" (1 Cor 2:7) that both Paul and John preached
as the wisdom of the spiritually mature. Such is the darkness of
our own intellectual abilities that a light of faith from the Spirit
of the risen Lord is required if we are to believe that God is not
only ecstatically in love with us in His constant self-giving, but
that He eagerly waits for our return of love.

John's world is quite radically different from the historical
accounts given of Jesus' life in the Synoptic Gospels. In the
latter, Jesus is actively engaged in preaching, teaching and
healing. In John, there is less action and more of longer discourses. Symbolic metaphors such as glory, truth, life and light
are used as John urges us to reflect on the meaning of Christ in
our daily lives.

John is a master storyteller. But the details — with some
core of historical tradition behind them — are not as important
as is the spiritual meaning set forth in symbols which usher us
into the hidden reality of the triune God's active presence in
this world. In a series of "I am" statements the Johannine Jesus
uses symbols of bread, water, light, life, vine, shepherd, etc. to

lead the reader into the various meanings hidden inside the reality of Jesus, the God-Man as He relates to us and to the material world.

SCOPE OF THIS BOOK

THIS IS not another exegetical commentary on John's Gospel with detailed explanation of each verse found in the Gospel. It is rather meant to be a source book for prayerful contemplation of the mystery of the indwelling Trinity within the individual Christian and within the Christian community at large.

I have chosen certain texts from John's Gospel which deal with the revealed dogma of God as a community of love made up of three distinct but inseparable Persons, Father, Son and Holy Spirit. It is primarily in this Gospel that Jesus reveals directly to His followers the ineffable mystery of the Divine Trinity and God's indwelling presence within the individual Christian and within the Christian community.

This doctrine — that God is one and yet also a loving community of inter-personal relationships of an I-Thou-We community — is central to our Christian faith. It not only reveals, through God's Spirit, the intrinsic make-up of God's family as Trinitarian, but it reveals to us and to the world which opens itself to the basis of all created reality that we are called to share in this very divine life, which John calls "eternal life."

Through abiding in the risen Jesus, God-Man, we also abide in the Heavenly Father and the Spirit. Such perfect love casts out all fear (1 Jn 4:18) and we in a continuous process become baptized, not only by water, but by the Holy Spirit (Jn 3:3, 5). We become beautiful children of God, capable of returning love for love.

Abiding in the Trinity, we are empowered by its indwelling omnipotence to work together as Jesus did with the Father in His Spirit of love (Jn 5:17) and to build other communities of love through service to all those in need.

SOURCES

I HAVE CONSULTED many of the classical commentators on John's Gospel of the early Church — Fathers such as Origen, John Chrysostom, Cyril of Alexandria, Augustine and Gregory the Great. Their commentaries are grounded in their *apophatic* theology. This theology recognizes that the human mind can positively come to some limited, yet, nonetheless, true knowledge about God and His relationships with the world which He created.

But the uniqueness of their theology lies in its teaching that we know God through a kind of *luminous darkness* (St. Gregory of Nyssa's term) of faith, hope and love which yields an experiential knowledge, a gift of the Holy Spirit "which is beyond all knowledge" (Ep 3:19).

I have also consulted the works of modern exegetes, including among many others the classic work on John's Gospel and Epistles by Raymond E. Brown in the Anchor Bible series, Vol. 29, 29A and 30. I found great help in the commentary of John J. Huckle and Paul Visokay in the Crossroad Series, Vol. 7, and the two volume commentary in the same series by Josef Blank, Vol. 8 and 9. Dr. William Barclay's two volume commentary, *The Gospel of John*; Vol. 1 and 2, added many background details as well as the commentary on John by James McPolin, S.J. in the series: *New Testament Message*; Vol. 6. I likewise received many theological insights from the the work of Paul-Marie de la Croix, O.C.D.: *The Biblical Spirituality of St. John.*

With such scholarly works to guide my thinking, I have sought to zero in on a very special point of view. Therefore, in this book I do not care to give a word-by-word commentary nor to engage in the problematic areas discussed so much better by "professional" exegetes, e.g. concerning the authorship of the fourth Gospel, the Johannine communities and their impact on Christianity, etc.

Concretely I have selected certain texts to lead the individual reader into a deeper contemplation of St. John's teaching on the indwelling Trinity. In each chapter I begin with a key sentence taken from a longer text of John's Gospel. I have sought to develop the meaning and applications of such a teaching in regard to our own personal, intimate prayer-life with the Trinity and in regard to an outward thrust to build a community of love out of the divinizing power of the risen Jesus' Spirit that should transform us into active children of God.

Each chapter ends with six additional texts that relate to the chosen one. These will provide further focus for one's deeper contemplation of God who is love. This is less a "book" to be read than it is an aid to contemplate the basic truth of Christianity, that God is one but also three, God is one nature but three loving Persons who receive their uniqueness as they live in self-emptying love for the happiness of the others.

May you remain united as the branch to Jesus, the Vine (Jn 15:4). May you continue to bear fruit as you experience the burning love of the indwelling Trinity within you.

Not that you chose me; no, I have chosen you
and the task I imposed upon you is to go forward
steadfastly in bearing fruit;
and your fruit is to be lasting.
Thus the Father will grant you any petition
you may present to him in my name.
This is all I command you: love one another   (Jn 15:16-17).

George A. Maloney, S.J.

St. Patrick's Novitiate
Midway City, CA.

Entering Into the Heart of Jesus

Meditations on the Indwelling Trinity in St. John's Gospel

1

"IN THE BEGINNING WAS
THE WORD . . . AND THE WORD WAS
GOD" (Jn 1:1)

JOHN BEGINS his Gospel as the Old Testament begins: "In the beginning. . . ." But the writer or writers of the Book of Genesis bring the reader to the first moment of creation. A spark exploded as it crackled and shot forth from the mighty heart of God. John, however, leads us beyond the first moment of material creation and places us, his readers, back into the very heart of God as a community.

God is "othering" Himself as He begets Himself and His Word from all eternity. The same presence of God as "kenotic" or self-emptying love — depicted in Genesis as a Spirit that hovers like a mighty cosmic bird over the chaos and the void — is hiddenly present as the bonding love between the Divine Mind and the Divine Word. John would soon reveal His name as the Holy Spirit.

Thus John wishes us to be grounded, if we are to become the community of God's love on this earth, in the very primal community of love, Father, Son and Holy Spirit.

3

Grounded in the Trinitarian community of love as the Source of all reality and life, John wishes to establish the Word's role, not only in human salvation, but also in the entire cosmos. He first establishes the eternal pre-existence of the *Logos*. At the beginning of time, when the material world first came into existence, this Word was in full being. The contrast between the changing, becoming, material, finite world and the unchangeable, ever-existing Divine Being, who is the *Logos*, could not have been produced more succinctly and effectively.

Other Johannine writings present the same idea of the pre-existent *Logos*. In the Book of Revelation, Christ is called the "beginning of God's creation" (Rv 3:15). He is "the Alpha and the Omega, the beginning and the end" (Rv 21:6; 22:13; 1 Jn 2:13-14). But the difference of emphasis between John's pre-existent *Logos* and the *Logos* of the sapiential literature of the Old Testament which gradually became the *Torah* (the Jewish Law personalized) is one of complete distinction by opposition.

This Law was the speech of God: "Thus says the Lord." But it remained always an *extrinsic* expression of the mind of God. John's choice of the word *Logos* is made to show precisely God's *immanent* relationship with the created world through the creative function of the Word. John is not interested only in telling us the nature of the Word; he wishes to tell us that the Word is pre-existent, abiding with God; hence of the same nature as God; therefore, "the Word was God."

God is! And out of God's immanent relationships of Father to Son and Son to Father through the Spirit of bonding love the uncreated, personalized energies of divine love explode into creation. This is essential to the Good News of John's Gospel: God who *is* from all eternity wishes to dwell in history. God who is immutable and independent in essence from all other beings freely moves into finiteness, into His material creation as the Source and Sustainer in whom all things have their being.

St. Irenaeus of the 2nd century beautifully describes this thought of John's Prologue as he writes that God creates this material world through His two hands, His eternal Son and the Holy Spirit. John writes of the creative function of the Divine Word: "All things came into being through him, and without him there came to be not one thing that has come to be" (Jn 1:3).

John establishes immediately a breathtaking perspective that covers the whole universe — of all that ever was, is, or ever will be. It is in the presence of the perfect Possessor of all being, God's creative Word and His Spirit of creative love, that we watch the created world slowly begin to move from the coldness of nothingness into the warmth of being. It is the Word that brings the universe from its existence in the mind of God into actual existence.

Thus for John, *Logos* is applied to Jesus Christ in His role of creating the total universe. It is not a static role that began once upon a time and is now finished. Wherever created beings are tumbling from the fingertips of God's inner being into existence or moving to a greater degree of existence or being, there the *Logos* is operative. For there can be no progression in being except through the *Logos* who is the Source of all being.

PRAYER

1. Jn 1:1-3
2. 1 Jn 1:1
3. Gn 1:1-4
4. Si 24:4-6
5. Heb 1:3
6. Ps 33:4-9
7. Pr 8:27-31
8. Is 55:10-11
9. Ws 18:14-19

2

"IN HIM WAS LIFE,
AND THE LIFE WAS THE LIGHT OF
MEN"   (Jn 1:4)

ALL OF US HUMAN BEINGS have a built-in hunger and passion to
possess more of life, more of *being* through a life of love for
God, the Absolute Beauty, and for all human beings. We
frenetically seek the Fountain of Youth which will conquer all
death and corruption. We seek elixirs that will give us more
"vitality" which is always connected with possessing "more of
life."

John has given us his view of reality, but it is seen from the
perspective of Jesus Christ, the glorified God-Man. In this view
God communicates His uncreated energies of love to us
through His Word, the *Logos*. He speaks to us through the
Logos and in that Speech we have our being (Jn 1:3; Col 1:16).
The abyss between God and nothingness is spanned through
the *Logos*. We find our whole *raison d'être*, our reason for
being, in and through God's Word.

St. Paul puts it quite succinctly: "We are God's work of art,
created in Christ Jesus to live the good life as from the beginning
He had meant us to live it" (Ep 2:10). When God's *Logos*
assumed flesh, our humanity, when He took upon Himself
matter, as eternally ordained by God in the total plan of creation, we and the whole material world were irrevocably called
to share in that life of the union of divinity and humanity. As
divinity and humanity were joined into being "without confusion," as the Council of Chalcedon (451 A.D.) described the

hypostatic union of Christ's two natures: divinity and humanity, so by analogy we and the world are joined together with divinity without confusion but in a unity of love.

John's Gospel views the beautiful diamond of God's infinite being as a community of burning, loving life seeking to share itself with "other-than-God" beings, i.e., the created world. If God is love by essence, then He is always seeking by His nature to share His being by communicating His presence. He is constantly calling us, who have been made according to His image and likeness (Gn 1:26), to share in His very own nature (2 P 1:4). In the Christian religion God becomes a God-toward-others by communicating Himself through His Word and His Spirit of Love.

God created the whole world as good, as a sign of His burning desire to give Himself in faithful communication through His Word. The world at its interior is filled with the self-communicating Trinity. God is filling the universe with His loving, triune life. His uncreated energies swirl through and fill all creatures with His loving, creative presence (Ps 33:4-9). God delights to give Himself through His Word to His creatures (Pr 8:29-31). Everything flows out of God's exuberant fullness of life and lives as a reality in His communicating Word. He speaks through His Word, and oceans and mountains, birds and beasts, flowers and all living things spring into being under His laughing, joyful gaze. Nothing that *is* can escape His loving, living touch, His active sharing as Giver of life. This God, as St. Paul preached to the Athenians, is not far from any of us, "for in Him we live and move and have our being" (Ac 18:27).

Not only does God communicate to His creation a sharing in His life, but He is a sustaining, directing God, leading us through levels of evolution as we cooperate with God, the Giver of Life, toward greater life. And so John tells us that God's *Logos* possesses life. And He comes to give us this life: "I have

come that they may have life and have it in abundance''
(Jn 10:10).

All life on any level of human existence is a sharing of
divine life through a participation in God's creative Word. We,
like fish, swim in God's ocean of illimitable life. John tells us
that God's creative Word is the bridge over which God's
shared life passes to us at every moment and in each human
situation.

God's fullest revelation of life-sharing is made in His incarnate Word, Jesus Christ. For in Him we have not only words
which communicate truths about God in His living relationships to His creatures but in the Divine Word made flesh we
have the dynamism of the Hebrew concept of Word, *Dabar*.
Besides concepts about God as life-giving, God's *Dabar* (or
Word) is the dynamic power that the Word releases in the
receiver of the Word. The Word is charged with creative power
and energy which flow from the Word into the receiver, transforming him/her — according to one's cooperation — into the
Word and the Mind that speaks the Word.

I AM
THE RESURRECTION AND THE LIFE

JESUS IS THE FULLNESS of God's life and He alone can give it to us.
This is the message found repeated over and over in John's
Gospel and in his First Epistle.

> . . . through the power over all mankind
> that you have given him,
> let him give eternal life to all those you have entrusted to him.
> And eternal life is this:
> to know you,
> the only true God,
> and Jesus Christ whom you have sent (Jn 17:2-3).

Knowing God is to enter into a whole way of life. It is the perfection or the completion of all other levels of human life, physical, emotional and intellectual. It is being caught up into a liberating, tender love of God toward each of us. This life is revealed to us through the spoken Word of God made flesh, Jesus Christ. "We can be sure that we know God only by keeping his commandments. . . . But when anyone does obey what he has said, God's love comes to perfection in him. We can be sure that we are in God only when the one who claims to be living in him is living the same kind of life as Christ lived" (1 Jn 2:3-5).

To be in God is to accept Jesus Christ as God's loving presence, which speaks continually — through His indwelling Spirit abiding in us (1 Jn 3:21) — of the Father's infinite love for us, even unto the death on the cross. God's life becomes our life in a prayerful experience of God's enormous love that frees us from narcissism and anxiety. Christ lives in us to the degree that we live as He lived, in self-emptying love for others.

St. Paul summarizes for us this new life that Christ brings us:

> As for me, by the law of faith I have died to the Law that I may live for God. With Christ I am nailed to the cross. It is now no longer I who live, but Christ lives in me. The life that I now live in this body, I live by faith in the Son of God, who loves me and sacrificed himself for me (Gal 2:19-20).

THE LIGHT OF MEN

GOD'S WORD BRINGS US God's life and divinizes us. It makes us children of God (1 Jn 3:1). To live in God's life is to live in the light of Christ's resurrectional presence and to be obedient to His inner direction, recognized by the indwelling Spirit.

Throughout the Old and New Testaments, including the writings of St. John, the theme of *light* is used in three ways.

First, light designates an essentially moral reality, a manner of upright living. John seldom uses the image of light in this sense. Except for a rare text, such as John 3:20, he is much too occupied with Christ as *the* Light.

Second, light designates an extrinsic rule of conduct, a norm for human actions. This is the usual way of referring to the Mosaic Law in the Old Testament.

Third, light designates Christ as the Messiah bringing salvation to those sitting in darkness or death. This third theme John employs in his frequent use of the word *light*. He applies it to Christ in His function as Savior, God's healing power among His children who live in darkness or the lack of God's life.

Christ in John's Gospel calls Himself the Light of the world, meaning primarily the one sent by God, who is God also, to bring us salvation: "I am the light of the world. He who follows me will not walk in the dark but have the light of life" (Jn 8:12). "I have come into the world as a light, so that no one who believes in me might remain in darkness" (Jn 12:46).

In the Prologue, John presents God's Word as Life that gives light or salvation. But sin has disrupted the plan of God. Not only mankind but the entire world is immersed in darkness. It is more than a mere absence of light. The darkness possesses an inimical force that rises up to extinguish the light. But already in the Prologue John predicts the victorious outcome of the Light conquering the darkness. "The light shines in the darkness, and the darkness did not lay hold of it" (Jn 1:5).

Nonetheless the fact that human beings failed to receive the Light did not lessen Christ's activity. He still remained the "true light" (1 Jn 2:8; Jn 1:9). Only Jesus Christ, not John the Baptist or anyone else, is the "true light" that illuminates all men. He is the true light because He is the Son of God, the true

Messiah, the Anointed One, who brings eternal life and truth to all who accept Him, His teachings and His person.

By use of the rich symbol of light, John pictures Christ not only as an illuminator, a teacher, but as the one who actually effects salvation. "He who follows me does not walk in darkness but will have the light of life" (Jn 8:12). The Light is at one and the same time the effect and the cause of the "life."

But not only will Christ's light of salvific action fall upon God's human children to divinize them by the indwelling, divine life of the Trinity, but He will save the whole universe, bathing it in a new light which will transform the world into the New Creation envisioned by St. Paul (2 Cor 5:17-20). In the Book of Revelation, John describes this universe which will be transfigured by Christ's salvific action into the Heavenly Jerusalem:

> The city has no need of the sun or moon to shine on it, because the glory of God lights it up, and the Lamb is its lamp. The nations will walk by its light and the kings of the earth will offer their tribute of recognition to it. . . . Night will be no more, and so they will have no need of the light of lamp or of sun, because the Lord will shine on them and they will reign forever and ever (Rv 21:23-25; 22:5).

PRAYER

1. Jn 1:4-11   3. Jn 11:25; Jn 6:48-51   5. 1 Jn 1:7; 2:9-10
2. Jn 5:24-25; 1 Jn 3:14-15   4. Jn 8:12; Is 9:1-6   6. 1 Jn 4:7-13, 16

3

". . . HE GAVE THEM
THE POWER TO BECOME CHILDREN
OF GOD" (Jn 1:12)

ST. IRENAEUS in the 2nd century summarized the aim of God's creation and the peak of its evolution when the Word became flesh: "God became man that man might become God." The early Fathers of the Church, especially those who wrote in Greek, following the Johannine and Pauline Greek texts, called this goal of the Incarnation *theosis* or *divinization*.

The presence of God's Word in Jesus Christ as the Light of the world does not coerce those who dwell in darkness to surrender to the Light and thus receive salvation. We find resistance in every atom of our being. Part of our unwillingness to let go and allow God to be sole Master within our lives comes from the state of disintegration in which we find ourselves. Through the contagion of collective sins, the result of the original fall, all of us now find ourselves disintegrated, not living according to our nature as God wants and has destined us to attain through His eternal Word.

The body now is a burden, something that brings us fatigue, suffering and pain. It is all too often an instrument of evil desires. The triple hierarchic harmony of body, soul and spirit has been broken. Endowed with freedom, we can so readily choose evil, unmindful of our true nature to be loving children of God who loves us infinitely. *Dipsychia* or double-souled is the term the early Christians (Jm 1:7) gave to this state of disintegration. St. Paul well describes it from his own personal observation: "... but I can see that my body follows a different law that battles against the law which my reason dictates. This is what makes me a prisoner of that law of sin which lives inside my body" (Rm 7:22-23).

REINTEGRATION

WE ARE helpless to heal ourselves and to make ourselves whole. St. John throughout his Gospel focuses upon this great pivotal truth. It is only through Christ, who is "the Way, the Truth and the Life" (Jn 14:6), that we can be restored to our primal dignity that God had intended for us when He said: "Let us make man in our own image, in the likeness of ourselves" (Gn 1:26). According to John, no one can come to the Father except through the Word incarnate (Jn 14:6).

It is He, Christ Jesus, who gives us the power to become children of God. He, who is God's Son by nature, through His Spirit released in fullness only when Christ died out of love for each of us, makes it possible for us to really become God's children by grace. The Incarnation for John is never considered an afterthought of God that attempts to save something of God's original plan which was frustrated through the sins of human beings. It is, rather, the culmination and visible peak of God's self-giving, passionate love unto death for each of us.

> So marked, indeed, has been God's love for the world that he gave his only-begotten Son: everyone who believes in him is not to perish, but to have eternal life . . . the world is to be saved through him. He who believes in him is not liable to condemnation, whereas he who refuses to believe is already condemned, simply because he has refused to believe in the name of the only-begotten Son of God (Jn 3:16-19).

This is, therefore, the *Way* to reach integration and fulfill God's plan for us, His children. The Word made flesh, true God and true man, "pitches His tent among us" only that we might accept His suffering, out-poured love, His Spirit, and receive in that infinite love the "power to become children of God" (Jn 1:12).

Typical of all the early Fathers in their understanding of the role of the incarnate Word is this statement of St. Maximus the Confessor of the 7th century:

> . . . it was necessary that He who is truly the author of creatures according to their nature should become also through grace the artisan of the divinization of those creatures in order that He who gave being should appear also as giving abundance of eternal well-being. Such is the work of the Word Incarnate. He has renewed the dispositions of nature and through His own Incarnation gave the gift of supernature, grace, divinization, to human nature.

INNER AWARENESS

BUT WE CANNOT RECEIVE salvation from Christ and His Spirit unless we discipline ourselves by an inner attention over the elements within us that tend to hold us in bondage and disintegration. We need, by God's grace, to come into that critical awareness which the Greek Fathers called *nepsis*. This means a "sober vigilance," an inner attentiveness to God's presence and a "passionate indifference," to quote Teilhard de Chardin, to seek always only what is pleasing to God. It is a mental balance, an internal vigilance and awareness of the movement of God's Spirit, leading us to true discernment of how we should react to any given situation or temptation according to our true dignity as God's loving children.

We are to live according to the *Logos*, the Light that brings us into true Life. Freedom becomes, ultimately, our choosing

always the good according to God's *Logos*. This true integration of ourselves according to the likeness of God is brought
about by fidelity to the interior living Word of God within us.
"Anyone who loves me will treasure my message, and my
Father will love him, and we shall visit him and make our home
with him" (Jn 14:23). "And this is the sum of eternal life — their
knowing you, the only true God, and your ambassador, Jesus
Christ" (Jn 17:3).

John will develop this truth about divinization stated here
in the Prologue. He reveals that it is only the Holy Spirit who
can assure us that we are united with God and truly growing in
greater loving union as His *real* children, insofar as we abide in
His only begotten Son, Jesus Christ.

The Good News that John holds out to us, viz. that we can
become, and hopefully already are, truly children of God by
grace through Jesus Christ, is beautifully summarized by St.
Symeon the New Theologian (+1022) who was so influenced
by John's writings.

> But, O what intoxication of light, O what movement of fire!
> O, what swirlings of the flame in me, miserable one that I am,
> coming from You and Your glory!
> The glory I know it and I say it is Your Holy Spirit,
> who has the same nature with You and the same honor, O Word;
> He is of the same race, of the same glory,
> of the same essence, He alone with Your Father
> and with You, O Christ, O God of the universe!
> I fall down in adoration before You.
> I thank You that You have made me worthy to know,
>   however little it may be,
> the power of Your divinity.
> I thank You that You, even when I was sitting in darkness,
> revealed Yourself to me. You enlightened me,
> You granted me to see the light of Your countenance
> that is unbearable to all.

I remained seated in the middle of the darkness, I know,
but, while I was there surrounded by darkness,
You appeared as light, illuminating me completely
     from Your total light.
And I became light in the night, I who was found in the midst
     of darkness.
Neither the darkness extinguished Your light completely,
nor did the light dissipate the visible darkness,
but they were together, yet completely separate,
without confusion, far from each other, surely,
     not at all mixed, except in the same spot where they
filled everything, so it seems to me.
So I am in the light, yet I am found in the middle of the darkness.
So I am in the darkness, yet still I am in the middle of light.

(Hymn 25)

PRAYER

1. Jn 1:12-13	3. Jn 12:24-26	5. Jn 17:22-26
2. Ep 3:16-19	4. 2 P 1:4	6. Jn 14:16-21

4

"AND THE WORD
BECAME FLESH AND LIVED AMONG US"
(Jn 1:14)

JOHN CONTRASTS our human birth as sons and daughters of God through the *Logos* with the human birth of the *Logos*, God Himself. In a few words filled with meaning he says: "And the

Word became flesh and lived among us" (Jn 1:14). By his choice of the word "flesh" (*sarx* in Greek), John is not thinking of Paul's contrast between spirit and flesh, the new and the old man. By use of this word, John strongly emphasizes the lowliness, weakness and temporality of man as opposed to the transcendence, power and eternity of the *Logos* who is God. Isaiah uses this contrast between "flesh" and the "glory of God" in a similar way:

> Then the glory of the Lord shall be revealed, and all mankind shall see it together; for the mouth of the Lord has spoken. . . . All mankind is grass, and all their glory like the flower of the field. The grass withers, the flower wilts, as the breath of the Lord blows upon it. So then, the people is the grass. Though the grass withers and the flower wilts, the word of our God stands forever (Is 40:5-8).

Flesh for John is everything that passes away, whereas the *Logos* is from all eternity, "before the beginning." There is no question in John's mind here of distinguishing between the divine nature of the *Logos* and the human nature that He assumed in the Incarnation. Rather, John is emphasizing the condition of the incarnational existence of the total, concrete person of Jesus Christ, the divine, eternal *Logos*, who humbles Himself to become "flesh"; the eternal becomes temporal, the unmovable becomes changeable, the Infinite becomes, before God, nothingness. We recall Paul's paean of praise to Christ who, being God,

> did not consider his equality with God a condition to be clung to, but emptied himself by taking the nature of a slave, fashioned as he was to the likeness of men and recognized by outward appearance as man. He humbled himself and became obedient to death; yes, to death on a cross. This is why God has exalted him and given him the name above all names, so that . . . everyone . . . should publicly acknowledge to the glory of God the Father that Jesus Christ is Lord (Ph 2:6-11).

GOD PITCHED
HIS TENT AMONG HIS PEOPLE

RESUMING John's Prologue, the Divine *Logos* left His heavenly state and took up His dwelling among us. John's thought here may have been inspired by the *Logos* personified in Sirach:

> In the highest heavens did I dwell, my throne on a pillar of cloud. . . . Over waves of the sea, over all the land, over every people and nation I held sway. Among all these I sought a resting place; in whose inheritance should I abide? Then the Creator of all gave me his command and he who formed me chose the spot for my tent, saying, "In Jacob make your dwelling, in Israel your inheritance" (Si 24:4-8).

As God stayed among His chosen people in the tabernacle of the Lord, so the Divine *Logos* pitched His tent or tabernacle and dwelled among the newly chosen people of Israel. John seems to follow, even in his choice of words, this cited passage. The Word that was with God from the beginning, that was active in the creation of the universe, now centers His presence in the tabernacle or temple of human flesh. John identifies here the pre-existing Word that created the universe and rules it by His power with the man of flesh that began to exist and whom John personally "had seen and touched."

Now all human beings have access to God's only begotten Son. The Word of God from all eternity has taken upon Himself our humanity. Divine Spirit is now human flesh. We can see Him through the faith of the early disciples who have seen and touched and heard Him. He does not put aside His divinity which He possesses as of the "same nature" (*homoousios*) as the Father. Rather, now we can rejoice with John and the early Christians to believe in the Good News of God's great love for us as to give us His Son (Jn 3:16) so that we — seeing Him through His teachings and actions, especially as He consummates His entire human life or mirrors the Father's eternal love for us by dying on the cross — can be drawn by Him to eternal life. Now, through John's witness, we Christians believe that God looks like Jesus. God acts as He acts. God relates to us as Jesus related to us. God suffers and dies in an analogous way for us as Jesus did on the cross. "My power is made perfectly evident in your weakness" (2 Cor 12:9).

"WE HAVE LOOKED UPON HIS GLORY . . . FULL OF GRACE AND TRUTH"

LOOKING ON JESUS through the testimony of the Evangelists, we now know what it means to be human. But it is also in Him and the way He lived His earthly life that we can understand what it means that God is acting in the lives of us modern-day people. In the New Testament He shows us an example of how human beings can live transcendentally by a love of self-emptying sacrifice on behalf of others. He lives for others. His focus is to bring fullness especially to the poor, the sick, the outcasts of society, the oppressed and the discriminated against, the criminals and the sinners. This is the way we should love. This is how we see the glory of God shining through us. God looks like Jesus! We will be like God if we live like Jesus!

John makes the transition from Jesus' humble state as "flesh" to the "glory" we have seen by means of a Semitic pun. In the Old Testament the dynamic presence of Yahweh in His awesome transcendence gives rise to His externalizing His glory, which is called *shekinah*. John, who writes his Gospel in Greek, nevertheless is thinking as a Jew and is fond often of linking, through parallelisms, the Old and the New Testament by drawing on images from the Old Covenant.

He chooses a form of the unexpected Greek verb *skenoun* which means "to tent" or "to pitch one's tent." The *s-k-n* consonants in Hebrew would convey to the Jewish mind God's *shekinah* or glory as externally manifested to human beings. It also stresses that the *Logos* has "pitched His tent," has become one among us in taking upon Himself our "flesh" or human condition. He is now the true Temple of God (Jn 2:19). There is no longer need, according to John's thinking, for restoring the Temple in Jerusalem which had been destroyed by the Romans in the year 70 A.D., for Jesus Christ is now the Temple wherein God fully resides and manifests His perfect glory among us.

"WHO SEES ME SEES THE FATHER"

THE GLORY of Christ's divinity shone through the frailness and lowliness of His humanity, by manifesting itself in His teachings and miracles. In His humanity there glowed the grace and the life of God. He touched men and women, looked upon them, spoke to them. His humanity was the point of encounter through which the life of God could flow into their lives. His sublime teachings, giving human beings the very mind of God Himself, were the light that turned them from the darkness of the ungodly and the perverse. The Incarnate *Logos* led them back to their Father by sharing with them the life and truth that was His.

PRAYER

1. Jn 1:14-18   3. Col 1:15-20   5. Jn 17:1-5
2. Heb 1:1-14   4. Ph 2:6-11   6. Jn 17:22-26

5

"SO MARKED, INDEED, HAS BEEN GOD'S LOVE FOR THE WORLD THAT HE GAVE HIS ONLY BEGOTTEN SON: EVERYONE WHO BELIEVES IN HIM IS NOT TO PERISH, BUT TO HAVE ETERNAL LIFE" (Jn 3:16)

THE FIRST MAN AND WOMAN conceived by God in the Garden of Eden are depicted as walking in His loving presence and communicating with Him in the coolness of evening. "He put his own light in their hearts to show them the magnificence of his works. . . . Their eyes saw his glorious majesty and their ears heard the glory of his voice" (Si 17:8, 11).

But man and woman lost the presence of God in their hearts. Instead of light, darkness and selfishness covered their innermost self. They lost consciousness of their true identity and their loving relationship to God. They had been created with a hunger for God's beauty. They were made according to God's image and likeness, "male and female he created them" (Gn 1:27). And thus there remains the terrifying searching in every person for his/her true identity, for a loving relationship with God's communicating presence, His Word made flesh, Jesus Christ.

No matter how much darkness covers our hearts, we seek frantically for a way out toward God's light. We sit in our isolated corners, sick, disturbed, lonely, angry and shivering from fright and meaninglessness. We have forgotten the language of communicating with God. Materialism has dried up our hearts and strewn the arid desert with tinsel and baubles, leaving us like discarded Christmas trees on a dump heap.

Yet God has not deserted His human children. He promises to cleanse them with clean water and give them a new heart. They can be "reborn" from above by God's Spirit of love and enjoy, even now, a sharing in God's eternal life! God has so loved His world that He sent — " from above," from within the very Trinity, the primary community of *agapic* or unselfish, self-emptying love for others, into our world of sin and death — His only begotten Son. God's face now has been "unveiled," revealed by His Word made flesh, Jesus Christ. "To have seen me is to have seen the Father" (Jn 14:9).

WHO DO YOU SAY I AM?

SINCE Jesus Christ's coming into our world, all human beings are forced to make a choice for or against Him as the only way to the Father and to true eternal life. Even a choice to remain in the darkness of ignorance or self-idolatry is to make a choice of sin or "unbelief" that is a rejection of God's truth. This truth is that He passionately loves His children and offers them in Jesus Christ true knowledge that is already eternal life (Jn 17:3).

John's Gospel has been called the *Book of Signs*. These signs are not only Jesus' miracles and healings, but also the miraculous events and actions of Jesus in His suffering, death, resurrection and glorification that invite all of us to believe He is Lord and God (Jn 20:29-31). They are signs opening all human beings to accept by faith that Jesus is the Messiah, the Divine Son sent to us by the Father to bring us "abundant life" (Jn 10:10).

Once God's Word became flesh and dwelt among us (Jn 1:14), the history of all human beings can be classified according to how we have responded to the "signs" given us in Jesus Christ. It is not so much that our historical time can be divided into B.C. (time before the Incarnation of the God-Man) and A.D. (the time after the Incarnation in "the year of the Lord"). Human history, in God's judgment, is measured by three possible responses to this person, Jesus Christ, and His signs or miracles that reveal His true nature.

Many human beings have responded down through the history which followed the coming of the Messiah, Jesus Christ, with no faith at all. In John's Gospel the Pharisees were representatives of such persons. "But although he had given such strong proofs of his claim under their very eyes, they refused to believe in him. Thus the saying of Isaiah the prophet was to be fulfilled: 'Who, O Lord, believed the message preached to us! To whom was the power of the Lord made known!' " (Jn 12:37-38).

In the encounter between Jesus and Nicodemus in our text we meet the second type of human response to the "signs" and person of Jesus Christ and His message. There is an honest, if tentative, searching out. As John characterizes Nicodemus, he "came to him by night" (Jn 3:2). He saw Jesus as a miracle-worker, a teacher of the law. He wanted to see whether Jesus confirmed the way he himself interpreted the law and the Jewish observances. "God is with him" (3:3) in the power of Jesus' words and deeds. But Nicodemus limits his response to his preoccupation with Jesus' signs and never moves to an authentic personalized faith. He never surrenders to the person of Jesus as the true Son of God.

The third class of people responding to the signs and person of Jesus embraces those who move into an authentic faith whereby they are born "from above," by water (Christian Baptism) and the Spirit, who gives them the gratuitous gift of faith to believe *into* Jesus as the true Messiah and the Son of God who brings salvation and healing unto eternal life.

FLESH vs. SPIRIT

JESUS ANSWERS Nicodemus' question of how to enter into the Kingdom of God. This concept of the Kingdom of God (or "of Heaven") is the central model of Jesus' parabolic preaching found in the Synoptic writers. John uses this term only twice as found exclusively in the dialogue between Jesus and Nicodemus. As typical of John's Gospel in the various "dialogues" or conversations between Jesus and various persons who seemingly are seeking a faith in Jesus, the listener, as here in the case of Nicodemus, misunderstands Jesus' words. Jesus is speaking on a higher level of faith, while Nicodemus crassly misunderstands the true meaning of Jesus' teaching.

The root source of conflict in understanding Jesus' teaching lies not in Nicodemus' materialistic understanding of Jesus' spiritual meaning. It lies in two different forms of understanding: that of a knowledge given in faith by the Holy Spirit and the other of a knowledge derived from a "fleshly" or "carnal" way of interpreting Jesus' words.

The Johannine Jesus is concerned with revealing the Kingdom to those open in childlike faith to receive the Spirit's gift of eternal life and regeneration through the Spirit by a rebirth as true children of God. "Jesus seized the opportunity and said to him: 'I must be frank with you: if one is not born anew, he cannot see the kingdom of God' " (Jn 3:3-4). Nicodemus totally misunderstands His meaning. He sees "birth" into the Kingdom of God as something physical. From his religious viewpoint Nicodemus could conceive entrance into God's Kingdom by being born into a Jewish family. The reward of Heaven would come in the heteronomous manner of obedience to God's authority by observing the laws of Moses and the external precepts of purification, prayer and sacrifice.

But Jesus is speaking of a rebirth that necessitates a faith-response to Him as the Way that reveals God's immense love for all human beings. John's Prologue prepares us to understand such a rebirth. "But to as many as welcomed him he gave the power to become children of God — those who believe in his name; who were born not of blood, or of carnal desire, or of man's will; no, they were born of God" (Jn 1:12-13).

The power to enter into an intimate sharing with the very Trinity of its divine life, Jesus tells us, must come from a source that is divine and of the Holy Spirit. A "rebirth" is necessary through God's power and not through any human doing to deserve or obtain it. John uses the Greek word *anothen*, which can mean "from above" (that which transcends all human power and resides in God's sole power to make possible) or "anew" or "again."

Because we human beings are "of flesh," we are locked into an alienation from God and condemned to a pitiable mortality or lack of every sharing in God's eternal life. We, through "sin" in our members (Rm 7:24), are tossed about by every selfish whim like flotsam on the ocean. We are in bondage to "fate" that holds us in captivity behind the prison walls built by our narcissistic selves. We are deaf to God's Word. We listen only to the importunate voice of our selfish egos.

BORN OF THE SPIRIT

THE *Pneuma*, God's breath which breathed physical life into us (Gn 2:7), is also His *wind* (*Pneuma* in Greek, *Ruah* in Hebrew) whose source is hidden and unknown by our human intellect alone, yet brings about new and dramatic changes which are the fruit of God's Spirit of love. *Pneuma* is also *spirit* which permeates all things. Thus God's gift of the Holy Spirit contains all three elements of breath, wind and spirit.

Jesus associates this regeneration with the Church's sacrament of Baptism of water, but also through a Baptism of the
Spirit through the infusion of faith, hope and love (3:5). Thus
the conditions to enter into God's triune community of love
and receive eternal life are to be born: from above anew, of
water through Baptism and of the Spirit through the gift of faith.

STAGES OF FAITH

FAITH, in John's Gospel, therefore, is never solely an intellectual assent to a truth revealed by God through the Church.
It is an existential encounter which moves us to a response to
the person of Jesus Christ. Through the faith-gift of His Spirit, we
Christians can accept, with absolute certainty, that He is the
perfect revelation in human form of what the hidden, unseen
Trinity is like. Jesus boldly claims that He has come from *above*.

He reveals to us what the real inner world of God as a
community of love looks like, because He is one of the members. He is the Son of God sent to this world of ours by His
Heavenly Father to reveal to us what He experiences from all
eternity in His intimate life with the Father in the same Spirit,
"who fathoms all things, even the depths of God" (1 Cor
2:10-11).

Secondly, Jesus at the peak of His revelation shows us that
it is His emptying love on the cross which brings about His
exaltation. "And just as Moses lifted up the serpent in the
desert, so the Son of Man must needs be lifted up, that everyone
who believes in him may have eternal life" (Jn 3:14). Jesus is
referring here to the loving concern of Yahweh toward His
people in the desert as narrated in the Book of Numbers 21:4-9.
Because of their complaints and lack of trust in God, Yahweh
punished the Israelites by sending them a plague of deadly fiery
snakes. They repented and God gave Moses — who had

interceded on their behalf — instructions to fashion a bronze serpent and set it on a tall pole. Whenever any were bitten by the deadly snakes, all they needed to do was to look up at the bronze serpent on the pole and they were healed.

The Son of man, lifted up on the cross, will be the source of healing and eternal life for those who look upon Him on the cross in faith. Christ, lifted up, is expressed in Greek by the word *hypsoun*. In John's mind this word conveys a double meaning. Jesus will be literally lifted up on the cross. But also the Son of God will be raised up in a glorious exaltation as the early Christian hymn expressed it, connecting Jesus' death with the resurrection:

> . . . Christ Jesus, who, though he is by nature God, did not consider his equality with God a condition to be clung to, but emptied himself by taking the nature of a slave, fashioned as he was to the likeness of men and recognized by outward appearance as man. He humbled himself and became obedient to death; yes, to death on a cross. This is why God had exalted him and given him the name above all names, so that at the name of 'Jesus' everyone in heaven, on earth, and beneath the earth should bend the knee and should publicly acknowledge to the glory of God the Father that Jesus Christ is Lord (Ph 2:6-11).

The death of Jesus on the cross calls to us for a response through the Spirit in faith that we believe Him to be the perfect expression of God the Father's infinite love for each of us unto death. Jesus perfectly reveals to us that God is love in His triune self-emptying gift to us of Father, Son and Holy Spirit, not only in His death but also in His glorification through His resurrection and ascension to the Father. There He intercedes for us for the release of His Spirit with the gift of faith which allows us to commit ourselves totally in a loving response to God.

So John breaks the dialogue between Jesus and Nicodemus to emphasize to the reader of his Gospel that in the death-resurrection of Jesus we have the ultimate revelation of the intensity of God's passionate love for us. "So marked, indeed, has been God's love for the world that he gave his only-begotten Son: everyone who believes in him is not to perish, but to have eternal life" (Jn 3:16). This entire world, not only human beings, but the total, material creation, is to be saved through Christ and not to be condemned or destroyed (Jn 3:17).

John adds that there are only two responses to Jesus Christ: one that brings, through faith in Him as the Son of God and revealer of God's love for us, a sharing in the Trinity's very own life; and the response of those who refuse to believe and are already condemned by their choice of not committing themselves to His revelation. Such bring themselves their own condemnation since they choose to remain in darkness even though the Light has come among them. "And this is how the sentence of condemnation is passed: the light has come into the world, but men loved the darkness more than the light, because their lives were bad. Only an evil doer hates the light and refuses to face the light, for fear his practices may be exposed. But one who lives up to the truth faces the light, so that everybody can see that his life is lived in union with God" (Jn 3:19-21).

This is the third level of faith that pushes us to "doing the truth." If Jesus is the full revelation of the Father, not only about the interior life of the Trinity, but also of the Trinity's self-emptying love in action for us in the order of salvation, then such a revelation, true teaching or orthodoxy (from the Greek word, *orthodoxia*, right teaching) given by the historical God-Man to us, calls for a faith-response in *orthopraxis*, or right living as a living out of the right teaching. To hear the Word teach us the truth about the Father's love for us and to turn away, preferring the darkness of self-centeredness instead of the light of Christ-centeredness, is to bring self-condemnation upon oneself.

Faith through the Spirit brings us into the Light of Christ and transforms us into the light of the world as we live our lives in complete oneness with the Lord. Anything else is a lack of a faith-response and is simply to remain in darkness and alienation from true and eternal life which is to know by faith the Father and Him whom the Father sent, *Jesus Christ* (Jn 17:3).

PRAYER

1. Jn 3:1-13   3. Jn 1:1-14   5. Ezk 36:16-38
2. Jn 3:14-21   4. 1 Jn 4:7-21   6. Ezk 37:1-14

6

"MY FATHER HAS BEEN WORKING TO THIS HOUR: AND SO I, TOO, AM WORKING" (Jn 5:17)

THE ESSENTIAL AND CENTRAL TRUTH that makes Christianity different from all other religions is its claim that the historical person of Jesus of Nazareth is both human and divine. He was born of a human mother and worked as a carpenter in His Galilean village. He preached publicly in Palestine, healed the sick and performed miracles. He was condemned by the Jewish religious leaders primarily for claiming to be the "natural" Son of God; therefore, divine. He was sentenced to death by crucifixion by Roman command. His intimate followers claimed He rose from the dead and the Heavenly Father glorified Him as His Divine Son.

There is no Christianity without the belief among Christians that Jesus is truly God, the Son of the Father, from all eternity. But He is also truly a human man. To this person God gave the power to bestow eternal life upon all who believed in Him as the Son of God. He is likewise empowered by God's Spirit to set up the milieu for the judgment and condemnation of those who refuse to accept Him as the full revelation of the living God made flesh.

St. Maximus, the outstanding Byzantine theologian of the 7th century, describes how Jesus Christ is the *Pontifex Maximus*, the greatest of all bridge-builders. He spans the infinite world of God (including the personalized world of the three Persons of the Trinity) and the finite world of mankind and created beings:

> We are astonished to see how the finite and the infinite — things which exclude one another and cannot be mixed — are found to be united in Him and are manifested mutually the one in the other. For the unlimited is limited in an ineffable manner, while the limited is stretched to the measure of the unlimited (*Epistola XXI*).

John the Evangelist presents us with a Gospel that bears witness to the oneness in nature of God the Father, Son and Holy Spirit. He selects "signs" or miracles with this in mind, to lead the reader to "belief" that Jesus is truly the pre-existent Word of God, made flesh, who dwelt among us as the imaged love of the triune God in human form. He is the only true *Way, Truth* and *Life* (Jn 14:6). He divinizes us by enabling us to share in the very life of the Trinity itself.

GOD'S AMBASSADOR

BEFORE WE PRAY out our chosen text (Jn 5:17), let us look at John's theological statement in John 3:31-36 that serves as a summary of what the Evangelist has already presented, especially in the first two "signs." It serves also as an introduction to the third sign, the healing of the invalid at the Sheepgate in Jerusalem and all that will follow in the remainder of the Gospel.

John 3:31-36 presents Jesus as the unique revealer of God's perfect love for us and the one who can bestow that divine life upon us since He is the only Son of the Heavenly Father. Whoever believes in Jesus and responds by a total commitment to Him hears God Himself. Jesus has the fullness of the Spirit to communicate the true words of God. And through the power of His Spirit, He, the Word-incarnate, is active and effective in that person's life.

> He who comes from above is above all; he who is sprung from the earth is earthly through and through, and his speech savors of the earth. He who comes from heaven is above all: what he has seen and heard — that is the sum of his testimony; yet no one accepts his testimony! Everyone who accepts his testimony thereby puts his seal upon the truthfulness of God; for he who is God's ambassador proclaims God's message; besides, he communicates the Spirit in no stinted measure (Jn 3:31-34).

Eternal life, which is to know the Father and the Son, Jesus Christ, through the Spirit's interior witness in the lives of believers (Jn 17:3), is already bestowed upon them as they believe in Jesus. "The Father loves the Son and has put all things at his disposal. He who believes in the Son possesses eternal life; he who refuses to believe in the Son will not see life. No, the anger of God lies upon him!" (Jn 3:35-36).

ONENESS
WITH THE FATHER IN ACTION

NOW WE COME to the third "sign," the healing of the invalid at the pool near the Sheepgate called Bethesda. Jesus heals the paralytic who lay thirty-eight years (a number to show how helpless and hopeless the invalid was to be cured) on his mat waiting for someone to bring him into the healing, bubbling waters of the spring. Jesus simply healed him, seemingly deliberately doing it on the Sabbath, and commanded him to pick up his mat and carry it home.

The legalistic Jewish religious leaders accosted Jesus and accused Him of violating the sacredness of the Sabbath. Jesus, as the Evangelist often presents Him, performs a miraculous healing and is challenged by Jewish religious leaders as to the source of His power. Then Jesus reveals something of His nature in relation to His Heavenly Father and of His power to give eternal life and judgment in the life to come to all who encounter Him in His revealed truth.

Jesus teaches His challengers what they already accepted in theory. "My Father has been working to this hour . . ." (Jn 5:17). The Jews of Jesus' time believed that God worked, even on the Sabbath. He brought life into being and He took such life away on the Sabbath. Jesus heals on the Sabbath because He is one with the Father. He always acts in all things dependently upon the Father. He enjoys absolute harmony in His oneness with the Father. ". . . and so I, too, am working" (5:17).

Jesus was not an automaton without free will, but in all things He turned inwardly to find His Father at the center of His being (Jn 14:11). There in the depths of His heart, His innermost consciousness, Jesus touched the Holy. He breathed, smiled, laughed and cried in the holy presence of His infinitely loving Father. All who came into contact with Jesus in new, surprising experiences, were touched by that delicate, sensitive gentleness. Absent was the slightest hint of aggressive autonomy and uncontrolled self-indulgence. Jesus was always present to the Father because the Father was always speaking His loving word in Him.

THE SON DOES
WHAT THE FATHER DOES

JESUS DOES what He sees the Father doing. "I tell you the plain truth: the Son can do nothing on his own initiative; he can only do what he sees the Father do. Yes, what he is doing — that, and nothing else, the Son does likewise" (Jn 5:19). If the Father is self-emptying love for the poor, the oppressed, the outcasts of society, the sick and the maimed, so Jesus also is. If one child, made by God according to His own image and likeness, is suffering on the Sabbath, the Father's compassion reaches out through the hands and lips of Jesus to give life and to pass judgment. St. Paul writes: "He (Jesus Christ) is the image of the invisible God . . ." (Col 1:15). Now Christians can believe in and commit themselves to Jesus Christ as the perfect reflection of the Father but in human form. His very being is God's revelation. "He who sees me sees the Father" (Jn 14:9). Looking up at Jesus — his blood poured out on the cross for us — we can believe that the Father also loves us in the same way because He and the Father are one. "Just as the Father loves me, so I love you" (15:9).

It is for this reason that the Jewish leaders accused Jesus of blasphemy. They understood by Jesus' justification of His working on the Sabbath to give new life to the invalid, that He was making Himself one with the divine nature of the Godhead. And yet their spiritual eyes were blinded to the oneness between Jesus and His Heavenly Father because they

lacked faith to accept the testimony of those who witnessed to
that divine oneness between the Father and His Son, Jesus
Christ (Jn 5:36-47).

MUTUAL KNOWLEDGE AND LOVE

JOHN THE EVANGELIST STRESSES throughout his entire Gospel that
Jesus and the Father are one, in being and in the actions which
flow from the transcendent, divine nature which is mutually
shared by the Father, Son and Holy Spirit. Therefore, Jesus in all
His actions looks to ("sees") the Father from whom He receives
the motivation for His actions, as in our text when He heals the
paralytic.

John makes special reference in this healing to the mutual
actions which the Father shares with His divine Son, in giving
new life and in judging. In them Jesus brings God's salvific
actions to the human race. Now we can know that God heals
us in our brokenness and gives us new life, that He is truly
Raphael, God who heals (Ex 15:26), because Jesus heals the
sick. We know that God forgives us our sins when Jesus says to
us in the sacraments of the Church words similar to those He
addressed to the invalid: "Listen; you are now well and strong.
Do not sin any more, or something worse may happen to you"
(Jn 5:14-15).

THE SON JUDGES
AS THE FATHER DOES

WE READ that the Father has given Jesus, His Son, the dual
power of bestowing eternal life upon those who believe He is
God's ambassador and of passing judgment. "Just as the Father
is the source of life, so, too, has he given the Son the power to

be a source of life; and he has authorized him to pass judgment, because he is a son of man" (Jn 5:26-27).

Yet there are Johannine texts which imply that Jesus has come, not to judge and condemn, but to save. "The fact is, God did not send the Son into the world to condemn the world. Not at all; the world is to be saved through him" (Jn 3:17). Jesus does not judge in the sense that He judges this or that action to be good or evil. He is the occasion whereby human beings are to be sifted, according to their own free choices in regard to their belief or unbelief in His person, seen in the final judgment as serving those in need or living only selfishly (Mt 25:31-46).

This sense is seen in Jesus' statement: " 'To be the parting of the way — that is my mission to the world: henceforth the sightless are to have sight, and those who see are to become blind!' Some of the Pharisees, who happened to be near, heard this and said to him: 'Maybe we, too, are blind, are we?' 'If you were blind,' replied Jesus, 'you would have no sin; as it is, you claim to have sight. Your sin remains' " (Jn 9:39-41).

Jesus is God's gift given to us unto eternal life. If any refuse to believe He is God's love incarnate, they condemn themselves. "He who believes in him is not liable to condemnation, whereas he who refuses to believe is already condemned, simply because he has refused to believe in the name of the only-begotten Son of God. And this is how the sentence of condemnation is passed: the light has come into the world, but men loved the darkness more than the light, because their lives were bad" (Jn 3:18-20).

JESUS' WITNESSES

THE LEGALISTIC PHARISEES would want to know who are the "witnesses" to Jesus since the Old Testament writers invoked the legal principle as found in Deuteronomy 19:15: "Whatever the misdemeanor, the evidence of two or three witnesses is required to sustain the charge." Jesus anticipates their thinking by freely offering the testimony of His "witnesses" to support His mission from His Heavenly Father.

Jesus offers four witnesses: (1) John the Baptist witnessed that he saw the Spirit of God in the form of a dove come down upon Jesus in His baptism in the Jordan. It is Jesus who will baptize with the Holy Spirit (Jn 1:19-34; 5:33-35).   (2) Jesus offers a "weightier" witness than that of John the Baptist. He appeals to His own works which are the continuation of Yahweh's works among his people (Jn 5:36).   (3) Next He appeals to a more subtle witness: that of the Father who bears witness to His Son's mission interiorly, in the hearts of those who follow His word as a rule of life (5:37).   (4) And, finally, Holy Scripture bears witness, especially the writings attributed to Moses, that Jesus' works are the fulfillment of their prophecies about the coming Savior (5:45-47).

Jesus' listeners in this scene, the Pharisees, represent the world of "unbelievers" who do not have the love of God in their hearts (Jn 5:42). Their desire to win the honor and approval of human persons makes them blind to God's glory and divine life present in Jesus. Jesus still asks us and all human beings throughout history: "Who do you say I am?" Everyone answers in one of two ways for no one can be indifferent to God's Word, His gift of life to the world: "You are the Son of God come to bring us eternal life" (Jn 3:16); or, "You blaspheme!"

PRAYER

1. Jn 5:1-18   3. Jn 5:36-47   5. Jn 9:1-41
2. Jn 5:19-35   4. Jn 3:31-36   6. Jn 17:19-27

7

"HE WHO EATS MY FLESH AND DRINKS MY BLOOD IS IN POSSESSION OF ETERNAL LIFE" (Jn 6:54)

WE KNOW that, once our parents have brought us into existence by God's providential cooperation, we will continue to *exist*, provided we have food, proper clothing and housing, etc. But we have been made by the triune God to move to higher levels of being human through the mystery of faith which brings us into vital, loving relationship with the triune community of love of Father, Son and Holy Spirit.

The work of the Divine Word incarnate, Jesus Christ, is to bring spiritual nourishment "for the development of your inner selves and to have Christ dwelling through faith in your hearts, and to be rooted and grounded in love" (Ep 3:16-17). For that reason John presents us with a powerful, symbolic sixth chapter to lead us away from mere physical existence into the realm of the mystical, the world of faith which only God's Spirit can open up to us.

Thus we see a typical unfolding of the dynamics repeated often in John's Gospel. In Chapter 6:1-13 we are given the account of the miraculous multiplication of the loaves and fishes (also found in Mt 14:13-21; Mk 6:32-44; Lk 9:10-17). The Jews were ready to accept Jesus as the long awaited prophet or messiah come into the world. They did not possess the Spirit's faith, but projected upon Jesus their desires to "exist" by the power of His miracles and never materially to want again.

Then John introduces us to the miracle of Jesus walking upon the Sea of Tiberias in the storm that filled the disciples in the boat with great fear for their lives. "It is I. Do not be afraid" (Jn 6:21). The other-than-human transcendence of Jesus was manifested to the disciples. Here John is leading us into the realm of mystery through faith in Jesus' divine power and oneness with the Father.

He exhorts the people who sought Him out in Capernaum: "You are looking for me, not because you saw manifestations of power, but because you partook of the loaves and made a hearty meal of them. Do not be concerned about the food that is bound to perish, but about the food that affords eternal life — the food which the Son of Man will give you; for on him God the Father has given his seal of approval" (Jn 6:26-27). Jesus invites them to have this eternal life. They are to believe in God's ambassador, Jesus Himself. The crowd indicated that it would believe in Him as the one sent by the Father if He would perform another miracle (and possibly many others without end!), comparable to the one which the great prophet of God, Moses, performed when he gave the people in the desert the manna from Heaven (Jn 6:30-31).

NOURISHING FAITH IN JESUS

THIS SETS the stage for the discourse of Jesus on the Bread of Life. The first part deals directly with faith in Jesus (Jn 6:35-50). Jesus is the Bread of Life that will nourish the crowd through faith and bring them into eternal life if they believe in Him as the Father's true ambassador, one in nature with Him. Jesus asks them to go beyond mere material bread and physical nourishment for a temporal existence which will be followed by death, and to seek a spiritual nourishment which is to be found in the mystery and meaning of His very person.

Jesus first teaches them that He is the spiritual nourishment that brings eternal life. Following Him cannot be within the compass of their own natural powers, but the Father must draw them by the Spirit's gift of faith.

> . . . My Father gives you the real bread from heaven; for only the bread that comes down from heaven for the purpose of giving life to the world is God's bread. . . . I am the bread of Life. He who comes to me will never hunger, and he who believes in me will never thirst. The pity is, as I said, you have seen me, and yet refuse to believe. Only one whom the Father entrusts to me will come to me; and when anyone comes to me, I will certainly not reject him; for I have come down from heaven not to do my own will, but the will of him whose ambassador I am: I must not lose anything of what the Father has entrusted to me, but raise everything from the dead on the last day. Yes, it is my Father's will that everyone who looks at the Son and believes in him shall have eternal life and be raised by me on the last day (Jn 6:32-40).

Jesus in this first part of His discourse on the Bread of Life claims that He is the food that nourishes faith and makes "divinization" possible. He is the one who reveals and shares with us God's gift of His very own triune, eternal life.

Revelation and nourishment, the Divine Word and Wisdom, are interrelated in the Old Testament. Such Wisdom is a gift of God and is of an experiential nature. Sirach presents Wisdom as the source of nourishment and life: "Come to me, you who desire me, and eat your fill of my produce. . . . Those who eat me will hunger for more, and those who drink me will thirst for more" (Si 24:19, 21-22). This nourishing Bread of Life is freely given to human beings by the Father as a gift and we can do nothing to acquire it beyond hungering and thirsting for it. "Nobody is able to come to me unless the Father, whose ambassador I am, draws him, that I may raise him from the dead on the last day. . . . Only he who has heard the Father's voice and learned the lesson comes to me. Not that anyone has actually seen the Father; only one has seen the Father — he who is here with authority from God. I tell you the plain truth: he who believes is in possession of eternal life" (Jn 6:44-47).

Thus Jesus insists that only faith in Him — by a committed response to His revelation that He has been sent by the Father as His ambassador to bring in His person a share of God's life — is the way to eternal life. Belief, as a power given by the Spirit to respond in complete commitment to the person of Jesus as the Son of God, is a gift from the Father through His Spirit. Such divine life is already enjoyed by those who believe in Jesus. Yet this eternal life will only reach a fullness when the Son of God raises up His followers "on the last day" (Jn 6:40).

THE BREAD FROM HEAVEN

THE FIRST SECTION, therefore, that deals with faith in the revelation and commitment to Jesus as being a nourishment, like bread, that transforms believers into divinized children of God, leads nicely into the second and main part of the discourse (6: 51-58). John makes the transition to specify that Jesus, as the Bread of Life, is most perfectly encountered as life-giving nourishment in the Eucharist.

Most commentators on John's Gospel agree on this from the internal evidence of words such as "flesh" and "blood" given by Jesus for the life of the world which recall the Synoptic writers' Last Supper account of the institution of the Eucharist. Thus many hold that this part of the discourse was probably originally part of John's Last Supper narrative, but was transposed later to fit into this discourse on faith in Jesus who is the Bread of Life. Faith in the person, Jesus, in His death and resurrection, and faith in the Eucharist can never be separated since they both deal with the same Jesus Christ. It is the same person who reveals Himself on the cross, through death, and through His Spirit once He is risen in glory, who nourishes us in the Eucharist with His total personhood as God-Man.

THE EUCHARIST

THERE CAN BE NO DOUBT that Jesus, in answer to the Jews' question, "How can this man give us his flesh to eat?", boldly repeats that He, in the gift of Himself as bread and wine, food and drink, is not speaking metaphorically, but rather existentially to mean an actual eating of His "flesh-body" and a drinking of His blood. He means literally to invite those who believe, not only to accept in faith His revelation, but also to encounter Him in the Eucharist in an actual eating and drinking of His total Self and thus be fully nourished into a sharing with Him of divine life.

From the text and the common understanding of commentators from the earliest times of Christianity, it is clear that Jesus is emphatically speaking about an actual eating and drinking, a participation in the Passover of the New Covenant in which He, the image of the Father, literally gives Himself as our nourishment unto eternal life.

> What I tell you is the plain truth: unless you eat the flesh of the Son of Man and drink his blood, you have no life in you. He who eats my flesh and drinks my blood is in possession of eternal life; and I will raise him from the dead on the last day; for my flesh is real food, and my blood is real drink. Whoever eats my flesh and drinks my blood is united with me, and I am united with him. As the living Father has appointed me his ambassador, and I live because of the Father, so, too, he who eats me will have life because of me. This is the bread that has come down from heaven. It is not what your fathers ate; they ate and died. He who eats this bread will live forever (Jn 6:53-58).

RECEIVING JESUS
WE RECEIVE THE TRINITY

THERE ARE many applications of the Bread of Life discourse to our own spiritual life. I would like to recall the underlying theme of this book of meditations, namely, the indwelling Trinity as seen through the Johannine teachings in the Fourth Gospel. Our centering in Christ and our entrance into the fullness of the Trinitarian life reach their peak of perfection in the Eucharist.

In the Eucharist we open ourselves to the ultimate presence of the uncreated energies of the personalized acts of self-gifting to us of the three Persons. It is Christ's resurrected body that comes to us in Holy Communion. But through this "Way," we are led into the holy presence of the Trinity. Now Jesus Christ, once He has "passed-over" in His death-resurrection and through the outpouring of His Spirit, can never be separated from His divinized humanity. It is the whole Jesus Christ that comes to us and this same glorified God-Man can never be separated from the Father and the Holy Spirit relationships.

In the Incarnation God so loved the world that He gave us His only begotten Son (Jn 3:16); out of this mystery of His infinite love for us flows the Eucharist. As the gift of the Eucharist is possible only because of the gift of the God-Man, the Logos-made-flesh in the Incarnation, so the mystery of the Incarnation leads us ultimately to the mystery of the Blessed Trinity. Who sees the Son sees the Father also (Jn 14:9). Who receives the body (John uses the Greek word, *sarx*, which means "flesh" and in Hebrew or Aramaic would be translated by "living human being") and blood of the Son of God receives not only the Son but also the Father in His Spirit of love. Who abides in the Son abides in the Father who comes with the Son and His Spirit to dwell within the recipient of the Eucharist (Jn 14:23; 6:57).

Thus all three mysteries of the Eucharist, the Incarnation and the Trinity are intimately connected and explain each other. The mysteries of the Trinity and the Incarnation are rooted in God's essence as Love. As the Trinity seeks to share its very own intimate, "family" life with human beings, made according to their own image and likeness, the Word leaps forth from the heart of the Father (Ws 18:14-15). Through the Incarnation all human beings are made one through the humanity of Jesus Christ. He is the *New Adam*, the true Father of the human race. We are destined to live with Him and through Him the very life that was of God's only begotten Son, which is the same eternal life of the Father and the Holy Spirit.

In giving us in the Eucharist his very body and blood as food and drink, Jesus Christ wishes to share with us His very own life, which is of the same nature as that of the Trinity (Jn 6:57-58). It is staggering to our weak human minds and impossible to comprehend adequately with the Spirit's faith the depths of God the Father's love for us as imaged in His only begotten Son. It is *in fact* that we become one with God's only Son. We are engrafted into His very being as a branch is inserted into the mainstream of the vine and becomes one total being (Jn 15:1-6).

St. John Chrysostom in the 4th century perceived this amazing mystery of our oneness with Jesus Christ which could serve as a fitting conclusion to this meditation:

> Therefore in order that we may become of His Body, not in desire only, but also in very fact, let us become commingled with that Body. This, in truth, takes place by means of the food which He has given us as a gift, because He desired to prove the love which He has for us. It is for this reason that He has shared Himself with us and has brought His Body down to our level, namely, that we might be one with Him as the body is joined with the head.

And to show the love He has for us He has made it possible for those who desire, not merely to look upon Him, but even to touch Him and to consume Him and to fix their teeth in His flesh and to be commingled with Him; in short, to fulfill all their love. Let us, then, come back from that table like lions breathing out fire, thus becoming terrifying to the Devil and remaining mindful of our Head and of the love which He has shown us (*Homilies on St. John's Gospel*).

PRAYER

1. Jn 6:1-23   3. Jn 6:35-51   5. Mt 26:26-29; Mk 14:22-25;
2. Jn 6:24-34   4. Jn 6:52-71   Lk 22:19-20; 1 Cor 11:23-25
                                               6. 1 Jn 2:20-29

8

"IF ANYONE THIRSTS, LET HIM COME TO ME AND DRINK" (Jn 7:37)

IN A WAY all of us are seekers like Ponce de Leon as we, too, try to find the fountain that will give us eternal youth. God has implanted in all of our hearts a passionate desire to possess a new and richer life, especially that beauty which will never change or perish. Jesus was no doubt appealing to this universal thirst for the fountain of eternal life when He cried out on the Feast of the Tabernacles in Jerusalem:

'If any man is thirsty, let him come to me!
Let the man come and drink who believes in me!'

As scripture says: From his breast shall flow fountains of living water.
He was speaking of the Spirit which those who believed in him were to
receive; for there was no Spirit as yet because Jesus had not yet been
glorified (Jn 7:37-39; *New Jerusalem Bible*).

John the Evangelist places this text in the dramatic setting
in which we find Jesus going up from Galilee to Jerusalem to
celebrate in the Temple the very popular feast of Tabernacles.
This beautiful festival each year recalled the time that the
Israelites had been homeless wanderers in the desert without a
roof over their heads (Lv 23:40-43). The Jews were to build
booths of temporary structure which would give protection
from the weather, but would not shut out the sun during the day
nor the stars at night. At the climax of this feast, a priest brought
a golden pitcher filled with water from the Pool of Siloam and
poured it out on the altar as an offering to God while the people
recited the words from Isaiah 12:3: "With joy shall you draw
water from the wells of salvation." The people thanked God for
life-giving water.

Besides commemorating the historical fact that the
children of Israel had been wanderers in the desert before they
reached the settled life of the Promised Land, it also was a
harvest-thanksgiving festival (Ex 23:16; 34:22), celebrated in
the autumn around October 15. It was popularly called "the
season of our gladness" since it marked the "ingathering" of all
the harvests of the land.

GOING HOME TO THE FATHER

IN THIS SETTING Jesus teaches in the Temple. Here we are again
given a typical Johannine example of Jesus' teaching, followed

by misunderstanding on the part of His listeners, and then His invitation to those who had "ears" to hear. John presents Jesus to us as one who invites us to share in the divine, triune life which He is offering to all who earnestly desire it. He again openly declares that He is one with the Father, who has sent Him to be His ambassador (Jn 7:28-29).

"My teaching is not my own invention. It is his whose ambassador I am. Anyone in earnest about doing his will can form a judgment of my teaching, to decide whether it originates with God, or whether I speak my own mind" (Jn 7:16-17).

He insists that He has come from the Father, who is His "parent" (Jn 7:28). In a little while He will return "home" to His Father (Jn 7:33-34). He enjoys an absolute oneness in nature with the Father. He is empowered, therefore, by the Father to teach with the Father's very own authority, an authority that is above even that of the Law given by God to His people through Moses. "I am not here by my own authority. No, in reality, I am but the ambassador of him whom you do not know. I know him, for he is the very one from whom I have come with a mission" (Jn 7:28-29).

He will soon leave their midst when His "hour" will come. That will happen at the time appointed by the Father to manifest the divine, triune community of love to the world when the Son of Man will be lifted up before the eyes of men and women. And only through the Father and Son's Spirit will those who are open to it receive the witness of the Father that, as the Father loves His Son, so the Son loves us (Jn 15:9).

LIVING WATERS

THEN AFTER HAVING TAUGHT during the middle days of the festival, "on the last and solemn day of the Feast" (Jn 7:17), Jesus stood up and invited the world to drink of the living water that He would give them. He had told the Samaritan woman: ". . . the water which I will give him will become in him a fountain of water welling up into eternal life" (Jn 4:14). Now Jesus was inviting all men and women to partake of the life-giving waters that would flow from inside them, deep down in the depths of their being, where the Holy Spirit of Jesus Christ would dwell. Jesus promises to the modern Christian who thirsts in the desert of his/her heart that He will put deep down into the very bowels of that person His Spirit of love who would lead all who responded to His call into a new knowledge and wisdom and understanding that Jesus is Lord and that with Him we have a loving Father who calls us to be sharers of the Trinity's very own divine life.

Scripture exegetes have offered two different translations of this text. The earliest and most ancient traditional understanding of, "from *his* breast shall flow fountains of living water" (Jn 7:38), stemming from the Asia Minor churches, presents Jesus as the one from whose breast shall flow fountains of living water. The other tradition, accepted generally in Western Christianity, holds that "He who believes in me will, as the Scripture has said, himself become a fountain out of which streams of living water are flowing forth."

In both cases there are truths expressed which John treats equally in other parts of his Gospel. St. Paul used the image of the rock that Moses struck. From it flowed forth living, life-giving waters which refer to Jesus Christ (Ex 17:6; 1 Cor 10:4). John links this tradition most likely with Jesus from whom will flow the life-giving waters of the Holy Spirit. In this passage he recalls to the reader's mind the out-pouring on this Feast of the Tabernacles of the life-giving water in the desert from the rock that Moses struck. Also John would present for our contemplation Jesus on the cross. His heart is pierced "and immediately there came out blood and water" (Jn 19:34). John is telling us that Jesus is the true Son of God who replaces the Jewish

Temple in Jerusalem. It is in this new temple that Israel shall worship because Jesus is the true source of real life for the whole world since He alone can reveal to us and make possible through the gift of His released Spirit the very in-dwelling Trinity of Father, Son and Spirit at the center of each of His true followers.

NEED TO THIRST FOR THIS LIVING WATER

IN BIBLICAL TERMS thirst for living water in the desert is a powerful image of the desire we should have to share in God's very own life. When this thirst is satisfied, when we are integrated into God, our potential for God is raised to a new ability to "absorb" God and be absorbed into His Being. We reach a point of equilibrium and of peaceful stability. The restlessness common to all human hearts that Augustine speaks about in his *Confessions* is put to rest only in God. And this very resting in God fosters new growth in Him.

It is the Bride, always losing the Bridegroom who, in her search, experiences her love for him growing ever greater in intensity. "By night on my bed I sought him whom my soul loves. I sought him, but I found him not" (Sg 3:1). Heaven will be the state of continuous growth in finding God in all His wonderful creatures and wanting to lead others to discover the same God loving them as well. Thirst is one of our most primitive experiences. Remove all drink from our lives and we will thirst and soon die. How better to describe our relationship toward God? We have been made to thirst for God. Yet God is always giving Himself to us through Jesus and the release of His Spirit to "drink." Jesus is always inviting all those who thirst, "Come to me and I will give you living waters." We come to know that to thirst for a greater union with the indwelling Trinity is unto our total health and happiness. The more we thirst, the more we can drink in the allness of God's goodness, beauty and very divine life, and the more also we should thirst to lead others to drink.

Thus in a way the second interpretation — that living waters flow from the bosom of the individuals who believe in Jesus as the Son of God — is also a correlate of the first interpretation. Louis Bouyer writes:

> The mysterious power of this water given by Christ is such that the one who has drawn at the fountain uncovers a fountain within himself. What he has drawn is divine life, love perpetually in act. He cannot have this love within himself, without loving; he cannot possess this gift, without giving himself and without discovering new possibilities of self-giving whose measure will be known only in eternity (*The Fourth Gospel*).

Before we can lead others to this "living water" that will take away any thirst for lesser goods, beauties and unsatisfying pleasures, we must first drink from it in our hearts that the desert of sin and our own poverty have raised to a feverish panting. We know, as we drink of Jesus Lord, that only in Him is true Life (Jn 14:6). We learn to die to self in a living baptism in which the living waters of Jesus Christ's Spirit of love surround us completely and heal us of all our ills. These waters of the Spirit refresh and give full life. Such a believer in Jesus then can bring the thirsty to drink of this same living water.

JESUS RELEASES HIS HOLY SPIRIT

JOHN USHERS US into the presence of the Trinity by likening the "streams of living water" to the Holy Spirit. "He meant by this the Spirit whom those who believed in him were destined to receive. As yet there was no outpouring of the Spirit, because Jesus was not yet glorified" (Jn 7:39-40). Jesus could not release

His Spirit, the Spirit also of His loving Father, until He had died. Why is this so? God's Spirit, like a gentle life-giving spring of fresh water in the desert, was always among men and women everywhere throughout God's creation.

But the Spirit could only become a cascading, mountain river, full and powerful, sweeping up all that the Spirit would meet and transforming it through God's own life when Jesus, the perfect human image of the Father's love for us, reached His passing-over from His self-possessed life to His life given for the life of the world.

THE PRESENCE OF THE HOLY SPIRIT

GOD'S SPIRIT OF LOVE was always present as God's transforming, loving power. But God is most "godly" when, as love, He is renewing through His Spirit His people by giving them a "new heart." God breathes His love into them. Repentance enables His people to open up to receive His breathing-in-Spirit of love and to become quickened again, to share life-giving relationships with the Trinity, Father, Son and Spirit. "I shall give you a new heart, and put a new spirit in you; . . . I shall put my spirit in you and make you keep my laws. . . . You shall be my people and I will be your God" (Ezk 36:26-28).

As we experience the continued gift of God's love poured into our heart by His Spirit, we begin to respond to our inner dignity as a child of God, loved infinitely by God Himself in the Father, Son and Holy Spirit. Sin and death lose their fearful hold over us, as we freely respond in love to become in every relationship with God and neighbor the unique, beautiful person God calls us to be. We are truly being reborn from above by the Holy Spirit (Jn 3:5)!

This Spirit who dwells within us reveals to us the living risen Lord as a dynamic, living Word guiding us to a new life befitting our dignity as children of God (1 Jn 3:1). Our Christian life is no longer one merely of observing laws, but now becomes a living response to the invitation of the Spirit to become what we really are in God's love. We respond to the living Word within us through the illumination of the Holy Spirit. We respond to the Spirit speaking from within us as well as speaking within the Church through its teachers, through its living tradition. We respond to the union with others experienced in the Eucharist as we live in the unity of God's Spirit of love.

We drink daily from the "heart" of Christ of these living waters of the Spirit which both flow from Christ and the Father but also from ourselves as we are constantly bathed in the waters of God's surrounding, renewing, life-giving love. All we need is to thirst for this living water and God will pour it out abundantly upon us and upon our world. This is the prophecy of Isaiah that is fulfilled in this text of John's Gospel:

> Oh, come to the water all you who are thirsty;
> though you have no money, come!
> Buy corn without money, and eat,
> and, at no cost, wine and milk.
> Why spend money on what is not bread,
> your wages on what fails to satisfy?
> Listen, listen to me, and you will have good things to eat
> and rich food to enjoy.
> Pay attention, come to me:
> listen, and your soul will live (Is 55:1-3).

PRAYER

1. Jn 7:1-31
2. Jn 7:32-53

3. Jn 4:1-45
4. 1 Cor 10:1-5

5. Is 55:1-3
6. Ps 63; Ps 42

9

"IF YOU MAKE MY TEACHING YOUR RULE OF LIFE, YOU ARE TRULY MY DISCIPLES: THEN YOU WILL KNOW THE TRUTH, AND THE TRUTH WILL MAKE YOU FREE" (Jn 8:31-32)

YOU AND I ARE more slaves than freed persons. Part of our slavery consists in having forgotten what true freedom as children of God means. We often are content to live in the narrow confines of our slavery, mainly because everyone else is in the same prison. Blindness would not be so great a suffering if all human beings were born blind and never could know any other possibility. But blindness would become un-bearable for all if there were even one man among them all who really could see!

The way we perceive ourselves, God and the world is pretty much the same way others perceive the same relation-ships. That is precisely part of our slavery. But Jesus Christ came among us with the eyes of God. He was one with the Father. He came to witness to the truth about God's community of love and told us that the Father and Holy Spirit love us with as much passion unto death as He, the Divine Word incarnate, loved us by dying for us on the cross. He was "the true light that enlightens all men" (Jn 1:9). That light shines in our darkness and cannot be overpowered by our darkness (Jn 1:5).

Like Lazarus, dead and in the tomb for four days before Jesus set him free, we too have been "entombed" in our slavery to sin and ignorance of God's truth. As Jesus wept for Lazarus in his death-condition, so Jesus weeps for us because He cares for us all. He enjoys the fullness of life since He comes from the Father, the Source of all life. He comes to give us a share in that fullness (Jn 10:10).

Yet, like Lazarus, how we live in the confinement of our own dark selfishness! We are not alive to God's truth. We are bound in so many ways and need to be set free by one who is freedom itself, Jesus Christ. Jesus wishes to come to us and address the same words He spoke at the tomb of Lazarus: "Unbind him, let him go free" (Jn 11:44).

JESUS, THE LIBERATOR

JESUS SPOKE of freedom and His ability to set us free in our chosen text: "If you make my teaching your rule of life you are truly my disciples; then you will know the truth, and the truth will make you free" (Jn 8:31-33). Rarely beyond these words however, does He speak formally of freedom. Yet His entire work of witnessing to the love of God the Father who sent Him to us was to set us free. He preached the coming of the Kingdom of God which in the Johannine Gospel means to live in the contemplation of the indwelling Trinity and to be transformed little by little into freed, loving children of God in our relations with other human beings as we build the community of love, the Church. He promised to send us His Spirit who would lead us into all truth.

Where the Spirit operates, it is unto true liberty. He frees us from our "carnal" way of judging ourselves and others and the entire world. He frees us from sin and guilt. His love in us drives away all fear. We become progressively more aware each day of our inner dignity as children of God. We begin to live on that deeper, interior level of communing with the indwelling Trinity.

Jesus' mission to bring us into the freedom of God the Father's children can be understood only in the context of love. But these two words: love and freedom, bring us into the basic, awesome mystery of the Trinity. In loving adoration the Holy Spirit speaks in the language of love which is silence. In silent awe before the majesty of God we rise above the relentless pull of time — past, present and future — to enter into the unchanging, uncreated energies of the Trinity. The love of God is poured into our hearts by the Holy Spirit which has been given to us (Rm 5:5).

In silence we learn how to love because in silence we receive God's infinite love for us. By letting go of our own concepts and ideas of God and in a searching cry to "see" Him in the way He wishes to reveal Himself to us, we enter into a new knowledge.

"I AM THE LIGHT OF THE WORLD"

IT IS, therefore, a preparation for Jesus' revelation of the truth about the community of God's triune love for us that He prefaces our chosen text on how He sets us free by His truth with a discourse about Himself as the Light of the world (Jn 8:12). Not only is Jesus, as we have seen in preceding meditations, the life-giving Bread from Heaven (Jn 6:25-59), and the life-giving Water (7:37-39), but now He reveals to us that He is also the life-giving Light (8:12). Whoever follows Him will not walk in darkness, but will have the light of life (8:12).

Jesus is the Light of God who dwells among us. He is God who brings us the true light of our salvation. "The light shines in the darkness, and the darkness did not lay hold of it" (Jn 1:5). Jesus alone is "the true light which illumines every man" (1:9). He is God's witness and revealer who shows us what God is like (14:9). Whoever accepts His revelation in faith is "saved," healed of all sin and unbelief (darkness), and enters into a life-giving relationship with Him and the Heavenly Father through the Holy Spirit (1:12-13; 8:25-30).

By His words and deeds, Jesus is the Light which reveals the eternal Father to us (Jn 17:3) and brings us Life. He makes it possible for us to become children of the light by becoming disciples of Jesus and living according to His teachings.

TRUE DISCIPLES OF JESUS

JESUS INSISTS that, if He is one with the Father, who has missioned Him as His ambassador to judge those who live in darkness and reject His witness to the Father's desire to share His triune life with us, then those who wish to walk in the life-giving light that brings salvation must "make my teaching your rule of life" (Jn 8:31).

John gives us in this brief passage the essence of what it means to be a disciple of Jesus. To be His disciples we need to "follow" Him by first accepting what He reveals as true. Belief is, therefore, the first stage in discipleship. But this means we must accept Jesus as the Son of God, equal to Him who is called "I Am who I Am" (Ex 3:14). Jesus is of the same nature as the Father. He is the only one who can say: "I *am* here — and I *was* before Abraham" (Jn 8:59).

We accept in faith that He has come as light to bring us life-eternal. His revelation is true. Therefore, His disciples must remain in His word or teaching. This means that we must listen with the ears of the "heart," an inner consciousness, permeated by the Spirit's faith, hope and love, to His revealed "words" or teachings.

The Greek word for disciple used here is *mathetes* which has as its root the verb *mathein* which means to learn. As disciples of Jesus we are to be inwardly attentive to Jesus continually speaking His revealed words to us. We are to learn, not only how Jesus lived according to values which most perfectly reflect the life of God's triune community, but also how we are to live in oneness with Him according to the same values.

If we live according to the values of Jesus, then indeed we "will know the truth, and the truth will make us free" (Jn 8:22). Such truth is more than mere truthful statements or logical reasonings. Jesus Himself is the Truth we are to "know."

GROWTH IN FREEDOM

By LIVING according to Jesus' light or revelation of God's truth, we will become "free." We will no longer be "the slave of sin" (Jn 8:35) by committing "sin" (which in John's Gospel means unbelief and rejection of Jesus as God's true ambassador). We will be sharers with God's only Son in God's household (8:35). "Consequently if the Son should make you free, you will be free in reality" (8:26).

THE FREEDOM OF JESUS

THUS JESUS COMES "to bring the good news to the poor, to proclaim liberty to captives and to the blind new sight, to set the downtrodden free" (Lk 4:18-19; Is 61:1-2). To see what our freedom in Him means, let us look at the freedom Jesus enjoyed.

The freedom of Jesus cannot be understood except in His relationship to His Heavenly Father. Jesus is perfectly free because at all times He turns inwardly and finds His Father at the center of His being. ". . . I am in the Father and the Father is in me" (Jn 14:11). He is surrounded on all sides and at His center by the surrendering love of His Father in total gift to the Son. Joy, ecstasy, peace and bliss pour over Jesus whenever He turns within and returns the gift of Himself to the Father.

Wrapped in the Father's consuming fire of love, Jesus could only whisper as He would during His public life: "Take all, Father, as You wish. I seek only to please You in all things." He knew, in the Father's great love, that He was His only Son. In that "eternal-now" gaze of the Father, Jesus continually sprang to new levels of awareness that He was sheer gift from the Father.

No separation could distance Jesus from the Father. He was always "at home" with the Father, "nearest the heart of the Father" (Jn 1:18). The Father rests in the fact that He has all His desires peacefully fulfilled in His Word through the love of His Spirit. Out of such unifying love, Jesus could move into the world of chaotic noise and activity, sin and separation and still be aware of His being God's Word.

His mission was to love, in that freedom, each person He met with the very love of the Father and thus bring the whole created world into a similar freedom. "As the Father has loved me, so I have loved you" (Jn 15:9). Jesus, in His prayerful immersion in the Father's loving embrace, was integrated and whole, freed from every estrangement from God and neighbor.

HE FREES US

JESUS' MISSION IS to free us through His revelation. This is the freedom that comes to us from the Spirit of the risen Jesus who frees us from isolation and brings us into a loving oneness in the Body of Christ (Ep 4:4). If we keep His commands, He and the Father will come and abide in us (Jn 14:23).

By His outpoured love, especially as shown on the cross, He frees us from all fears. How often in John's Gospel Jesus invites the disciples not to be afraid but to accept His peace. "It is I. Do not be afraid" (Jn 6:21; Rv 1:18). "Peace be with you" (Jn 20:20). We need never fear again, for the risen Jesus has conquered sin and death and He lives in us (1 Jn 3:24). "You have in you one who is greater than anyone in this world" (1 Jn 4:4).

He frees us from ourselves in our darkened self-centeredness by being our inner life and the image according to whom we have been created by God. He frees us from all sin, especially the root of all sin, which is unbelief in Jesus' true nature as the Son of God and in His truthful revelation of the Father's infinite love unto death for each of us.

Freedom is, then, actually the love of God working within us to empower us with a self-sacrificing love for others. It gives us the ability to take our lives in hand and return them to God by living every thought, word and deed according to Christ, God's *Logos* or Word, in whom all things have their being. We become liberated as we exist on ever new levels of consciousness of this oneness with all in Christ who is one with the Father through the same Spirit of love. Freedom brings us joy and the exciting desire to become ever more and more the whole universe as we experience a new capacity of *being* from their love returned. Ultimately Heaven or the Kingdom of God is that state of inner freedom where we allow God's love, the Trinity, to recreate us ever anew as His children and to send us out to love one another in His love. When we love one another, not only is God's love being perfected (1 Jn 4:12), but our freedom as a disciple of Jesus is manifested. We are becoming free indeed! (Jn 8:36).

PRAYER

1. Jn 8:12-20   3. Jn 8:31-36   5. Rm 5:1-11
2. Jn 8:21-30   4. Jn 8:37-59   6. Rm 6:1-11

10

"I HAVE COME
THAT THEY MAY HAVE LIFE AND HAVE IT
IN ABUNDANCE" (Jn 10:10)

IN HIS INTRODUCTION to the works of William Blake, the poet
Yeats wrote: "We perceive the world through countless little
reflections of our own image." Blake himself complained that
the majority of human beings cannot stand much of "reality"
so they learn to create worlds of illusion to escape hard reality.

But Jesus comes "from above," from the very heart of the
Father, into a world of spiritually dead or dying human beings
and promises to bring them life, but life more abundantly. Yet
our images and the illusions which we create in order to hold
on to our false securities and not "pass-over" to embrace this
new and eternal life offered by Jesus Christ prevent us from a
true conversion toward a fuller life. We believe in certain things
about Christ and His message. We fail to believe *in* Him.

Jesus makes the lament of the prophet Isaiah His own as
He castigates the religious leaders of His times because they
allowed the sheep to go astray for lack of a good shepherd:

> Your ears will hear,
> yet you will not understand;
> your eyes will look
> yet you will not see.
> For blunted is the sense of this people:
> their ears are hard of hearing,
> and their eyes are shut;

thus neither their eyes see,
nor their ears hear,
nor their minds understand;
and they are not converted and healed by me
                              (Mt 13:14-15; Is 6:9-10).

If we were Jews in the time of Jesus, what impression would His message and His works have made upon us? Holding tenaciously to the monotheism of Judaism, we too would have wanted to know whether His claims to be the Son of the Heavenly Father were the product of sheer madness or was He really the expected Messiah. Those who were open to His message hoped that He might, indeed, be the long-awaited Messiah, but they usually had a much different, selfish view of what they expected the Messiah to bring them by worldly power. Others, particularly the Pharisees and the Scribes, asked Him who He was (Jn 10:24), not because they were inclined to believe in Him, but because they wanted to trap Him in blasphemy.

It is difficult for us today to understand how revolutionary Jesus' claim to be the Son of the Heavenly Father was. It meant that He was empowered by the Father to perform great healings and miracles, but, above all, to bestow eternal life upon all who believed in Him. Jesus had told only two persons in John's Gospel that He was the Christ, the Messiah: the Samaritan woman at the well of Jacob (Jn 4:26) and the blind man (Jn 9:37). But in our selected passage for meditation on the parable of the Good Shepherd Jesus speaks in parables of shepherd and sheep and then, by way of explanation, boldly declares His oneness with God. It would be for this and for no other reason — namely, that the religious leaders of the Jews clearly understood that Jesus was making Himself one in authority and power with God — that according to their law, He had to be put to death for blasphemy: "Not for a kindly deed do we mean to stone you, but for blasphemy and because you, a man, make yourself God" (Jn 10:33).

Jesus is claiming that He alone has the fullness of God's life and that He has been sent by the Father to share it with us. But to prepare His audience to accept Him as the Giver of eternal life, He speaks in several parables which center mainly around the pastoral themes of the relationships between shepherds and their sheep.

THE TRUE SHEPHERD

IN THE FIRST PARABLE Jesus claims, against the false shepherds or teachers of the Jewish religion, that He is the true shepherd since He enters into the sheepfold through the door. The keeper of the sheepfold recognizes Him as the true shepherd and opens the door for Him, while the false shepherds, the Pharisees and Scribes to whom Jesus is addressing this parable, are described by Jesus as those who act like thieves and robbers and enter into the sheepfold by some other way (Jn 10:1-6).

Jesus characterizes Himself as one whose voice the sheep recognize and readily follow. They truly belong to Him. He marches before them. There is an intimate relationship between the sheep and the true shepherd.

In the second parable Jesus likens Himself to the door through which the sheep enter. All will go well with the sheep who go in and out through Jesus since He, as the true shepherd, leads them to green pastures (Jn 10:7-9). It is in this context of the second parable that Jesus makes His bold statement that whoever follows Him will have abundant life: "I have come that they may have life and have it in abundance" (10:10).

THE SOURCE OF LIFE

THIS THEME of Jesus as the source of life is an essential one found repeated in John's Gospel: ". . . everyone who believes in him is not to perish, but to have eternal life" (Jn 3:16). Other texts are found in John 3:36; 5:40; 6:33, 35, 48, 51; 14:6; 21:31. We have already seen elsewhere how John presents Jesus as the "living water" (4:10), the "bread of life" (6:35), the source of "living water" (7:38) and as the "light of life" (8:12).

Here, Jesus uses the pastoral image that had a long history in Old Testament literature to describe the religious and political leaders of Israel as shepherds (cf.: Gn 31:39; 1 S 17:34-37; Ps 23:1-4; Ex 2:16; Jr 2:8; 3:15; 10:21; Ezk 34:3-23). A parallel to Jesus' contrast of the false teachers of His time and His own goodness as the one empowered by the Father to bring the sheep to true pasturing that would give them eternal life is found in Chapter 34 of Ezekiel.

Yahweh is impatient with the false shepherds who govern His people. He takes His flock back from them and declares:

> I am going to look after my flock myself and keep all of it in view. As a shepherd keeps all his flock in view when he stands up in the middle of his scattered sheep, so shall I keep my sheep in view. I shall rescue them from wherever they have been scattered during the mist and darkness. I shall bring them out of the countries where they are; I shall gather them together from foreign countries and bring them back to their own land. . . . I shall feed them in good pasturage. . . . There they will rest in good grazing ground. . . . I myself will pasture my sheep, I myself will show them where to rest. . . . I shall look for the lost one, bring back the stray, bandage the wounded and make the weak strong. I shall watch over the fat and healthy. I shall be a true shepherd to them (Ezk 34:11-16).

How accurately is this a description of the God-Man's mission! He was sent by the Father to His people to bring them abundant life.

DIVINE LIFE

WHAT IS THIS ABUNDANT LIFE which Jesus, the Good Shepherd, comes to bring us? John gives us the pithy statement, repeated often in his Gospel, that Jesus Christ is the love of God incarnate, come to this world so that we who would believe in Him would have abundant life. "So marked, indeed, has been God's love for the world that he gave his only-begotten Son: everyone who believes in him is not to perish, but to have eternal life" (Jn 3:16). The parable of the Good Shepherd is Jesus' way of describing how He comes in self-sacrificing love on behalf of His sheep to lead us into this divine life, which is to know the Father and His Son, Jesus Christ (Jn 17:3).

But to describe this divine life in which we are called to be participators (2 P 1:4) leads us into the very mystery of God Himself as a community of Persons sharing the life of each other. The Good News Jesus brings us is that God is both one and also a community or family of loving Persons. God is one nature, equally shared by three Persons in an ecstatic, loving intimacy of a Father emptying Himself into His Son through His Spirit of love. Such intimacy and self-emptying are returned by the Son gifting Himself back to the Father through the same Spirit. In the Trinity Jesus reveals to us the secret of divine life.

Love is a call to receive one's *being* in the intimate self-surrendering of the other. In the ecstasy of "standing outside" of oneself and becoming available through the gift of love to live for the other, the Father and the Son and the Holy Spirit all come into their unique *being* as distinct, yet united Persons.

Christianity teaches us, in the fundamental truth about the Trinity, that at the heart of all reality or true *being* is the Spirit of Love that is calling two Persons into intimate "ecstatic" communion with each other. In joyful surrender the two discover their uniqueness in their oneness. Their presence to each other as gift, a giving way in free self-surrender of each to the other, paradoxically is a receiving of new life, new openness, that yearns still more to live as gift to the other.

EXPLODING LOVE OUTWARD

OUR FAITH ASSURES US that such ecstatic love of the Trinity explodes through the same Spirit of Love to embrace a created world in the passionate desire to share the triune, divine life with others. St. Irenaeus of the 2nd century describes us human beings as "empty receptacles" to be filled by God's goodness. How exciting and yet how humbling to realize that we, along with the whole material creation, are caught up into the Trinitarian ecstasy of love! We are a part of God's joyful discovery of what it means to be uniquely a Father toward a Son in the Spirit of Love.

The presence of each Divine Person to each other is similar to their presence to us. As the Father is turned toward the Son in total openness, availability, vulnerability unto complete self-emptying, so the Son is turned in the same Love, the Spirit, to the Father. That ecstatic "turning" to each other is the same when they turn in love toward us. God has created us out of His ecstatic happiness that we might live in ecstasy, too, in a "going out" of ourselves and moving always in loving presence toward others.

St. Paul beautifully captures the same vision as that found in John's Gospel as he describes our predestination to enter into the very divine life of God:

> Before the world was made, he chose us, chose us in Christ, to be holy and spotless, and to live through love in his presence, determining that we should become his adopted sons, through Jesus Christ. . . .

And it is in him that we were claimed as God's own, chosen from the beginning, under the predetermined plan of the one who guides all things as he decides by his own will; chosen to be, for his greater glory, the people who would put their hopes in Christ before he came (Ep 1:3-12).

THE GOOD SHEPHERD

HOW DOES JOHN DESCRIBE for us the love which empties itself from within the triune community of love? He tells a parable, a graphic, symbolic way of speaking about the very mystery of God's love and burning desire to share His very life with us. This is the power of the Gospel parables. God's mystery is closed to human reasoning and logic. It is "unveiled" to the humble and poor of heart who come to *know* — in the sense of the Semitic word, *Yada* — and to *accept* Jesus as "one with the Father."

The "sheep" that belong to the Good Shepherd experience, in the love of their Pastor, the outpoured love of the Heavenly Father through their mutual love, the Holy Spirit. The Spirit makes Jesus known to His disciples as the image of the Father's passionate love unto death.

Jesus is not only the true and only shepherd who leads us into the sheepfold, the Kingdom of God. He is also the *good* (in Greek the word is *kalos*, indicating a gentle, loving, self-sacrificing kindness) shepherd. He "lays down his life to save his sheep" (Jn 10:11). He knows each of us in our unique personhood, by our *name*. And by the Holy Spirit, we know Him as the only begotten Son of the Father. As the Father loves Him, so He loves us unto death (Jn 15:9).

ABUNDANT LIFE

WE ARE PRIVILEGED to receive a share in God's very own existence as we accept the works Jesus does as proof that He has
been sent by the Father to give us this eternal and ever more
abundant divine life. Jesus on the feast of the Dedication in
Jerusalem — which annually celebrated the restoration and
reconsecration of the Temple under Judas Maccabee (1 M
4:59) — revealed His credentials as the Giver of Life. This feast
was also known as Hanukkah or the Festival of Lights. John
presents Jesus in this setting as the Light of the world.

He has already presented Jesus as the new Temple of God.
Perfect praise and glory to God are now centered in this person,
Jesus. He alone pleases the Father. He fulfills the wish of the
Father that He manifest to us, by His death and resurrection,
God's immense love for us. And He makes this abundant life
possible to us through His released Spirit of love.

Jesus simply testifies to His works as signs of His oneness
with the Father. "The things I am doing in the name of my
Father testify in my behalf" (Jn 10:25). He insists that the Father
and He are one (10:30). But no one can accept this unity of
nature unless the Spirit of the Heavenly Father draw him. One
of the ways this happens is through the works that Jesus does.
"If I do not act as my Father does, then do not believe me; but if
I do, then believe on the strength of my actions even if you do
not believe my words. Thus the truth will dawn on you, and
you will understand that the Father is in me and that I am in the
Father" (10:37-39).

Jesus' argument that He and the Father enjoy the same life
and that Jesus can, therefore, give this life to the world is that He
shares the same works with the Father because they both have
the same divine life. The works of Jesus in the Gospel are never
His own personal works, but are always seen as revelatory of
the work the Father does. But the greatest work of Jesus will take

place on the cross in His hour of greatest manifestation of the passionate love of the Father and the Son through the Spirit of love for all of us, God's children.

We contemplate the Word of God made flesh in Jesus, emptied out on the cross to reveal to us that God looks as Jesus does. God the Father does the same work of loving us even to the madness of giving His very own life to us for our eternal happiness. We are called to be transformed by this same life within us, and to go forth and do "works" as Jesus does, as a result of our communion with Jesus and the Father in their mutual Spirit of love (Jn 14:12; 3:19). This is our continued response to the three divine Persons revealing themselves in Jesus. The proof that we are children of God and have been transfigured by God's love is seen in the "works" we do in self-emptying love for others, since we do works similar to the Father and the Son. We, too, really share their divine life!

PRAYER

1. Jn 10:1-10   3. Jn 10:22-42   5. Ezk 34:11-16
2. Jn 10:11-21   4. Jn 14:6-15   6. Ps 23

11

"I AM THE RESURRECTION AND THE LIFE. HE WHO BELIEVES IN ME WILL LIVE EVEN IF HE DIES" (Jn 11:25).

BEFORE WE COME TO JESUS' "hour" when in His passion and death He revealed Himself in His humanity as divine love poured out unto the last drop of water and blood for us, John presents us with the very significant story of Jesus' raising Lazarus from the dead. We have been stressing so far that Jesus Christ for John is the full and perfect revelation and interpreter of the Heavenly Father through the faith-understanding given to us by the Holy Spirit.

As man, Jesus, in His human words, gestures, deeds and, above all, sufferings, makes God intelligible to us. As the eternal Son of God, He opens us up through His Spirit to an unending, unlimited understanding of God's self-revelation as self-emptying love for each of us. Jesus in His human nature is not revealing so much His own nature as He is the total revelation of the Father. He is the *LIFE*, sharing in the same nature of divine life with the Father. He is the *WAY* that brings us into a real sharing in the divine, Trinitarian life through His being also the *TRUTH*. He reveals in His personhood what He summarizes in the statement: "Of his own accord the Father loves you dearly, because you are settled in your love for me and in your conviction that I come from the Father" (Jn 16:27-28).

The Evangelist John prepares us for the ultimate enunciation of the paradox that Jesus, dying, will live forever. In His risen form, He is the endless revelation of God's infinite love for us. As a prelude to the great and conclusive *Act* of Jesus on Calvary, John tells us the story of the death and restoration to life of Jesus' dear friend, Lazarus.

DYING, WE LIVE

LIKE A POWERFUL SYMPHONY, John, in this narrative, continually develops the leit-motiv that will become clearest in Jesus' death on the cross. The paradox is that He is *Life*, and yet He freely dies so that we who are born into the death of not sharing in the triune life of God may participate in that divine life and live forever, even if we should all die physically.

The English poet, Francis Thompson, restates in his provocative *Ode to the Setting Sun* the paradox that runs through this eleventh chapter of John's Gospel.

> For there is nothing lives but something dies,
> And there is nothing dies but something lives.
>   Till skies be fugitives,
> Till Time, the hidden root of change, updries,
> Are Birth and Death inseparable on earth;
>   For they are twain yet one, and Death is Birth.

Jesus' raising of His physically dead friend, Lazarus, back to life is the sixth and final sign in John's Gospel. By this miracle Jesus reveals that, because He is one with the Father, He has the power to raise up all human beings to share in the same divine life (Jn 11:23-26; 12:18). By raising Lazarus from the dead, Jesus wishes to teach that He is the "Life" of God held out to each individual Christian and to the entire Christian community if they "believe" in Him as truly the Son of God.

John also makes this miracle the sign of Jesus' approaching resurrection and His empowerment by the Father to bestow that *life* on all who believe in Him (Jn 11:25). Yet Jesus' new life can come only through His final and greatest revealing sign, His death on the cross (Jn 12:32). And yet this very raising of Lazarus, as John presents it, is the final *sign* that will move Jesus' enemies to seek His condemnation and death (Jn 11:53).

Here we are confronted once again with the paradoxical connection between faith-belief and unbelief. In the very revelation by Jesus that He possesses life-giving power over eternal death, the "unbelievers" decide to take His earthly life by inflicting physical death upon Him through crucifixion.

The pivotal truth of the Lazarus story, explained in paradoxical terms of life and death, is that whoever believes in

Jesus as the Son of God, even though he/she physically dies, shall live forever. *Life* and *death* have for Jesus (and, therefore, should have for all Christians) a higher meaning than the merely physical. The central point is that whoever is a true believer in Jesus need never fear physical death, for eternal life has been given to them in their ongoing belief-response to Jesus as the true revelation and interpretation of God's truth.

Eternal life in the spiritual sense is "knowing" the Father and His revealing Son, Jesus (Jn 17:3). True and ultimate death is the sin of unbelief in Jesus shown in an obstinate rejection of Him as the full revealer and interpreter of God as a triune community of love.

DO YOU BELIEVE THIS?

JOHN PRESENTS MARTHA, the sister of Mary and Lazarus, as typifying Christian believers in Jesus who see Him as a powerful intercessor before the Father, but not fully as God Himself with power to bring us into eternal life. "Martha said to Jesus: 'Master, if you had been here, my brother would not have died. And even now I know that whatever you ask of God, God will grant you' " (Jn 11:21-23).

It is to such as Martha that Jesus reveals that He is the resurrection and the life. Whoever believes in Him will live forever (Jn 11:25-26). She makes a firm act of faith in the Messiahship of Jesus and attests that He is "the Son of God who was to come into the world" (Jn 11:27).

Martha brings to Jesus, Mary, the symbol of the Christian who sits lovingly at the feet of the Lord and receives His words on the deep spiritual plane. She is accompanied to Jesus by her Jewish friends who, with her and Martha, mourn the loss of Lazarus. Here we see the most human traits of Jesus depicted in John's Gospel. The sight of Mary and her friends weeping at the loss of Lazarus touches Jesus profoundly in the depths of His being. "The sight of them stirred Jesus deeply and shook his inmost soul" (Jn 11:33).

Jesus stands before Lazarus' tomb and lifts His eyes to His Heavenly Father. "Father, I thank you for listening to me. For myself, I knew that you always hear me; but I said it for the sake of the people surrounding me, that they might believe that I am your ambassador" (Jn 11:41-42).

Jesus thanks the Father. There is given no concrete petition by Jesus to the Father. His prayer is a triumphal revelation of His oneness with the Father in the mutual Spirit of love.

THE GLORY OF GOD

JOHN OFTEN SPEAKS as he does here (Jn 11:41) of "the glory of God." This is the "Kabod Yahweh" or the glorious presence of God made visible through His deeds of power. In the Old Testament we see this "glory" of God as power unveiled in fire, lightning, thunder, etc. In John's Gospel Jesus is the glory of God made visible on earth. ". . . and we have looked upon his glory — such a glory as befits the Father's only-begotten Son — full of grace and truth!" (Jn 1:14).

Through Jesus' deeds of power, "He revealed his glory, and his disciples believed in him" (Jn 2:11). In our text John refers to two different levels of glory. "Did I not tell you that if you have faith, you will see the glory of God?" (Jn 11:40-41). Immediately Jesus is referring to the power He possesses from the Father because He comes from Him and is of one nature with Him as the mutual Giver of life and the Conqueror over the evil powers of death, sin and unbelief. John also means to open the reader to the final glory of Jesus when He returns triumphant to the Father. Eternal life is given to His humanity by the Father, who in the resurrection raises up His Son to that oneness which was His from all eternity in His divine nature. Through *His* glorification, humanity is exalted and enters into the very Trinitarian life of God. God's very own glory is now more clearly manifested in the divine-human love-sacrifice of Jesus than that glory ever was revealed before the time of the incarnation, death and resurrection of the Word made flesh.

JESUS, LIFE-GIVER

JESUS HOLDS out to each of us the possibility of sharing God's eternal life. As Jesus raised Lazarus to new life, so we too, through selfless obedient faith, can be set free by Jesus and given eternal life. "Unbind him, let him go free" (Jn 11:44).

In contemplation, God's Spirit is communicated to us directly, without words or images of our own choosing and to the degree that we have purified our hearts of all self-centeredness. Like Lazarus, we are always coming from the darkness of our dead selves into the light of Christ's presence. We discover in adoring that loving presence throughout the day, in the context of each moment and of each event, that we are free persons in Christ.

Jesus entered into each moment during His earthly life with maximum freedom. He took His life and gave it back joyfully to His Heavenly Father as gift for gift received. So, likewise, freed Christians live freely by taking their lives into their own hands and determining each thought, word and deed according to what would most please the Heavenly Father. "Nothing lives but something dies . . . nothing dies but something lives."

PRAYER

1. Jn 11:1-16	3. Jn 11:38-57	5. Jn 12:20-36
2. Jn 11:17-37	4. Jn 12:1-11	6. Lk 10:38-42

12

". . . AND NOW HE GAVE THEM THE GREATEST PROOF OF HIS LOVE" (Jn 13:1).

WHEN JESUS GATHERED HIS FRIENDS, the disciples, together for a last meal, He is described as having great excitement in His heart. He is nearing "His hour," the hour for which the Word became man and dwelt among us. Everything from the cave of Bethlehem, the small home in Nazareth, the desert temptations, the previous few years of exhausting travels to preach and to heal the multitude led to this moment.

> The feast of the Passover was now approaching, and Jesus knew that his time for passing from this world to his Father had arrived. He had always loved his own who were in the world; and now he gave them the greatest proof of his love (Jn 13:1).

Periodically during His public life this flaming love in His heart to accomplish what His Father had sent Him to do would flare out in words of ardent longing. "I have come to bring fire to the earth and how I wish it were blazing already! There is a baptism I must still receive, and how great is my distress till it is over." (Lk 12:49-50). "Now is the sentence of condemnation being passed upon this world; now is the prince of this world being evicted, and I, once I have been lifted up from the earth, will draw all men to myself" (Jn 12:31-32).

His hour would be His baptism in the Spirit of God's infinite love for Him in His humanity. Through Him God's love would be manifested to all of us as water and blood poured out from His loving heart, the heart of the suffering, triune God, imaged in the humanity of the suffering servant on the cross. When the spear would open His heart and there would pour forth the last drops of water and blood, and there would be nothing held back, then Jesus' work would be consummated. "It is now completed" (Jn 19:30).

What is completed? the Greek word John uses for "It is finished" or "It is done fully or perfectly" is *tetelestai*. Thus John conveys the idea that Jesus' death, the end of His earthly work, is ended, finished, but that it also embraces His "new creation," His resurrection, and this is the completion or perfection of God's plan for the world: ". . . that through him God should reconcile to himself every being, and make peace both on earth and in heaven through the blood shed on the cross" (Col 1:20).

GOD'S KENOTIC LOVE

GOD IN MAN HAS NOW FINALLY SPOKEN His definitive Word in Jesus Christ. St. John, standing at the foot of the cross, has nothing more to tell us. He invites us to "see" the Word being spoken clearly, telling us at that moment of God's infinite love for us. The horrendous folly of the sufferings of Christ is sheer nonsense except in terms of the logic of divine love! For the contemplative Christ, poor in spirit, the terrifying *kenosis* or self-emptying, even to the last drop of blood and water, has fullest meaning only in being an exact *image* of the heart of God the Father in His infinite, tender, self-sacrificing love for each of us. "He who sees me sees the Father" (Jn 14:9).

To prepare us to understand the full meaning of the sacrifice of Christ on the cross leading to His resurrection and the victory of life over death for each of us if we accept to imitate Him, John presents us with the powerful, symbolic action of

Jesus' washing the feet of His disciples. It is a concentrated summary, not only of the way Jesus chose to live in loving service on behalf of the poor and broken ones of this earth, but also of the way the Trinity lives in self-emptying love for us.

John points out that the washing by Jesus of His disciples' feet shows Jesus' superiority over them and His supreme freedom which prompted Him to perform the humblest task of a slave so that His disciples and those who would follow them would "know" how great is His love for them. St. Peter does not understand the significance of Jesus' actions but Jesus explains: "What I intend to do you do not understand right now, but you will understand by and by" (Jn 13:7). Peter and other Christians would understand only through the outpouring of the Holy Spirit after Jesus' death and resurrection.

And that understanding would embrace two truths absolutely essential to living the true Christian life. The first is that Jesus shows that He in human form images the triune God from all eternity in choosing a life of loving service on behalf of others. God's love for us is a "kenotic" or self-emptying love. Such a love Jesus images by His total availability, His mutuality in sharing Himself as our equal, and His complete gift of Himself unto death.

What is God like? He is like Jesus. How does God love us? He loves us in the way Jesus images that perfect love for us. In the Last Supper Jesus opens His loving heart to His disciples. It is a humble heart that wants to serve as a slave. Jesus bends down and washes the feet of Peter and John, Judas and the other disciples. The heart of God never bent lower to touch His children than in that gesture of humble service. The primary meaning of this gesture, beyond the example Jesus gives for His disciples' imitation, is that He is the image of God's divine power placed at the service of us human beings. "My Father goes on working, and so do I" (Jn 5:17).

In the early Christian hymn quoted by St. Paul (Ph 2:6-10), Jesus — one with God — did not deem this an honor to hold on to but "He emptied Himself." Jesus did not give up His divinity in becoming man, but, more positively, He became a most perfect expression of it. He reveals that at the heart of all reality is the triune community of loving Persons who live for the others. It is a community of an *I* and a *Thou* in a *We* community, constituted by the bonding, hidden love of the Spirit. It is based on *ek-stasis*, the ecstasy of standing outside of or beyond the self-control of oneself in order to move toward others in self-giving. It is to be "othered" into new levels of personhood by living for the other. It is emptying love which brings true fulfillment as the gift of oneself comes back to birth the giver into true *I-ness* through the gift of the beloved.

TRINITY AND UNITY

IF JESUS IMAGES the type of love the Father has for Him within the Trinity, then we can understand in the mystery of the Trinity that the Father does not exist independently of the Son, nor the Son and Spirit independently of each other and the Father. There can be no Father except through the *kenotic*, self-emptying love of the Father for the Son in the Spirit of self-gift. There can be no Son existing within the Trinity independently of His essential relationship to the Father who begets Him eternally in and through His Spirit of self-emptying Love.

If the intimate, Trinitarian relationships between Father, Son and Holy Spirit are the same relationships of the triune God toward us, His human creatures, who share in His image and likeness, then we should accept the foundational position that God truly relates to us in the self-emptying gift of Himself to us in Jesus Christ as a suffering servant. God is supremely *relative*, the one always turned toward others in serving love.

WE SHOULD BE
TURNED TOWARD ALL OTHERS

OUT OF THIS TREMENDOUS, active, creative, self-giving love of the Trinity, living within us, we are to be transformed by so great a love of God, Father, Son and Holy Spirit, to live for others. Thus the action of Jesus washing the feet of His disciples goes far beyond any ritual, liturgical action we are to perform annually. It even goes far beyond ourselves imitating Jesus by seeking to perform the most menial tasks for others. Its power lies in the symbol of how we also, to the degree that we have been transformed by the self-emptying love of the triune God, as manifested by Christ and recognized by the outpouring of the Spirit, must live for others in a similar *kenotic* love. This is the way we prove to others we have become truly children of God, that we *can* love others as Jesus, the Father and His Spirit love us at all times and in all events of our human lives.

Jesus chose the symbol of washing the feet of His disciples with water to indicate a complete, comprehensive cleansing of all our worldly values to live as Jesus lived. We are able to understand the meaning of Jesus' death:

> But if we shape our conduct in the atmosphere of his light,
> as he himself is in light, we have union with one another,
> and the blood of Jesus, his Son, cleanses us from every
> stain of sin (1 Jn 1:7).

The saving death of Jesus would bring us a total cleansing from all sin that comes from self-centeredness, driven by power to dominate God and neighbor. His blood cleanses us. It is an active symbol of how great God's love for us is. In Jesus Christ, God shows how much He wishes to be a suffering servant on our behalf. If we could contemplate this *kenotic* love of the triune God who dwells within us, truly the blood of Christ would cleanse us from "every stain of sin."

And the proof, not only that we are disciples of Christ, but that we truly have been "saved," must lie always in the readiness we have to give away our beautifully transformed selves in humble, loving service to others in utter *availability, mutuality* and *self-gift*. God's perfect, active love for us is seen at work when Jesus makes Himself the Servant of us all, not only in washing our feet but in shedding His blood. Jesus experienced the complete outpouring love of the Father through His Spirit and He chose a human style of life that best reflected His return of love, or better, the transformation He experienced in becoming — through the Father's love — His beautiful, beloved Son.

So, as we experience the infinite, emptying, serving love of the indwelling Trinity for us, we too should live for others in self-sacrificing service. Following Jesus means to be washed thoroughly of all our desires for power and domination to live as He lived: as a suffering servant.

PRAYER

1. Jn 13:1-20   3. Jn 15:9-17   5. Mt 25:31-46
2. Ph 2:1-11   4. Jn 19:31-37   6. Lk 22:24-30

13

"LOVE ONE ANOTHER AS I LOVE YOU" (Jn 13:34)

YOU ARE FAMILIAR with the technique of "flashbacks" used in movies, plays and novels. A "flashback" is an interruption of a chronological sequence of events in a literary work with the interjection of events of an earlier occurrence. In meditating on the farewell discourses of Jesus, the flashback technique can help us to understand the Evangelist's meaning.

Apparently the writer and his hearers were not contemporaries of the historical Jesus. They belong to His community, the Church which has handed down to them a right teaching (*orthodoxia*) about the historical Jesus who died and arose and was exalted and glorified by the Father. It is, therefore, the glorified Christ who is speaking to the Christian community through faith and love in an historical setting.

This is the "kairos" or the *now* moment that reveals the identical same person to be the historical Jesus and the Christ of faith (experienced in the community's preaching, faith, prayer and the communal celebration of the Lord's Supper) as well as the "Son of Man" who will appear in the ultimate future.

Faith, therefore, for John is the overlapping of the past and the future in the present moment, in which the community in the "now," through faith and in love, meet the earthly and glorified Jesus as the same Christ of faith.

John uses the apocalyptic title from Daniel of the "Son of Man" to refer not only to Jesus as the revealer of God but as the one who is at the same time the historical Jesus and the Christ exalted in glory through the resurrection, who now lives in His Body, the Church.

GLORIFICATION
OF GOD AND OF JESUS

JESUS IN HIS FAREWELL DISCOURSES SPEAKS often of the *glory* or glorification of His Father, of Himself and of His disciples. The Greek word *Doxa* (in Hebrew: *Kabod*) is found often in

Scripture with various meanings or associations. It can refer to divine light and glory or the splendor and radiance of God. At times it can be associated with the clarity and power of God's revelation or to the bestowing of prestige or reputation upon another.

When John uses this term, *glory*, he is suggesting a sharing through participation in the divine realm of being. This is the divine sphere of God's activity and life in contrast to the world's darkness and lack of glory. Revelation for John is the principal role of Jesus as the one who "unveils" by revealing the divine glory of God's presence in the world. ". . . and we looked upon his glory — such a glory as befits the Father's only-begotten Son — full of grace and truth!" (Jn 1:14).

John is telling us that this historical man, Jesus of Nazareth, through His death on the cross and His resurrection, has been "glorified," that is, He has left this world and has been lifted up. He has ascended into the divine realm of the Trinity. He came from this realm and *now* He returns to it.

His disciples cannot go with Him at that historical moment. ". . . where I am going, you cannot come" (Jn 13:34). He will go to prepare a place for them and will come back to take them "home" with Him (Jn 14:3-4).

Jesus is "glorified" by God who witnesses through the Spirit of the Father that Jesus is the definitive Revealer and Savior of the world. But the Father also is glorified in His Son who reveals the full nature of God. The divine realm Jesus reveals to His followers is that God is a community of loving Persons, Father, Son and Holy Spirit. God is love, each member living in self-emptying love for the other.

LOVE ONE ANOTHER

AND THAT IS THE NEW COMMANDMENT Jesus gives. John does not repeat the double commandments of the Old Testament (Dt 6:6; Lv 19:18) or the same given by the Synoptic writers (Mk 12:28-34; Mt 22:36-40; Lk 10:25-28). Jesus, according to John, gives us a "new" commandment. It is simply "to love one another as I love you" (Jn 13:34). The applications to God, neighbor and the entire world are measureless! But such a love is meant by Jesus' revelation to be reciprocal, a love of self-giving that transforms and comes back to the one who first loves.

This can be done by Christians only through the knowledge of Jesus' love as revealed by His Spirit, given in fullness only when Jesus has died (Jn 7:39-40). The manner in which Jesus loved us by dying on the cross is the norm for Christians in their mutual love for each other and the whole human race. This love partakes of the dimension of a missionary witness. "By this token (sign) all the world must know that you are my disciples — by cherishing love for one another" (Jn 13:35).

Such a love has an eschatological aspect for it reveals the loving and caring involvement of God toward His created world. It is this "perfect" love of God that is moving to final completion in the *Parousia*. This divine love, which abounds in the hearts of Christians through the Holy Spirit (Rm 5:5), gives Christians strength to live in faith and love in all their actions.

FAITH AND LOVE

THE KEY ELEMENTS that permeate and give direction to the Christian's life are faith and love. "God is love and he who abides in love abides in God and God in him" (1 Jn 4:16). It is a radical call to let faith in God's self-giving love in Jesus on the cross permeate every facet of our human living to the point where we practice a similar self-emptying love toward others.

John's First Epistle best summarizes this new and radical commandment, based on faith and love.

> This is precisely the message which you have heard from the beginning — that we should love one another. Be not like Cain who was a child of the evil one and murdered his brother. Why did he murder him? Because his own life was wicked, whereas his brother's was holy. Do not be surprised, brothers, if the world hates you. We know that we have passed from death to life, because we love our brothers. He who does not love abides in death. Everyone who hates his brother is a murderer, and you know that no murderer has eternal life abiding in him.
>
> We know what love is from the fact that Jesus Christ laid down his life for us. We, too, ought to lay down our lives for our brother. How, then, can the love of God abide in him who possesses worldly goods, and, seeing his brother in need, closes his heart to him? Little children, let us not love merely in word or with the tongue, but in action, in reality.
>
> . . . We also receive from him whatever we ask, because we keep his commandments and do what is pleasing in his sight. His commandment is this, that we should believe in the name of his Son, Jesus Christ, and love one another, as he commanded us. He who keeps his commandments abides in God and God in him. It is the Spirit abiding in us who gives us the assurance that God abides in us (1 Jn 3:11-24).

PRAYER

1. Jn 13:31-38	3. 1 Jn 4:7-21	5. Jn 15:12-17
2. 1 Jn 3:11-24	4. 1 Jn 5:1-12	6. Jn 17:20-23

14

"I AM THE WAY"
(Jn 14:6)

TRUE RELIGION IS ALWAYS CONCERNED with the fundamental question of human meaningfulness. Your favorite dog or cat cannot sit
in the corner and ponder its destiny, its goal in life, and decide on
the means needed to attain that goal. But this is precisely what
makes us human beings superior to all other sub-human creatures. We *can* reflect on the purpose or goal for which God is
continually creating us. And we can freely, without extrinsic
coercion, determine the means to attain our end.

God has implanted deeply within us certain "archetypal"
experiences which become actuated through the use of symbols,
matter and form, sacramental signs of word and action, which
lead us into the experience of what the symbols stand for in the
archetypal order.

John is a master in choosing universal symbols that resonate
in the lives, experiences and desires of all human beings. We all
possess a universal, human longing for the beautiful, the true, the
"real life," which will never end.

John links up the meaning and goal of our existence and
deepest longings with the historical but eternal, human but divine
person, Jesus Christ. John's Gospel continually presents his faith-
vision of Jesus, which was the same for all Christians of the first
century, as the ultimate source and the perfect means for all
human beings whereby they could attain salvation or eternal life.
Encountering Jesus as the complete *Revealer* of the Father in His

earthly activities, death and resurrection unto "glory," we have
the way to God and the means to attain full human meaningfulness.

"I AM"

IN NO OTHER Old or New Testament writings do we find so
many of the "I am" formulas as we find in John's Gospel. These
sayings are of two kinds: those that are without a predicate and
those that are completed by a predicate or symbolic term
which open us up to new and deeper ways of understanding
the person of Jesus Christ and His message.

The first class is John's favorite way of describing the risen
Lord as the pre-existent Word made flesh, of one nature with
the eternal God, who possesses the very authority of God
Himself simply because He is truly God. All such "I am"
Johannine formulas take the reader back to the Old Testament
texts where "I am" without a predicate is the simplest
shorthand to express God in His absolute "I-ness," in His utter
transcendence, independence and self-commitment.

This is seen in the famous text of Exodus 3:14: "I am who I
am." It is often expressed in Deutero-Isaiah, as for example:

> "In you are my witnesses," says the Lord, "and my servant whom I have
> chosen, that you may know and believe me and understand that I am
> he. Before me no god was formed, nor shall there be any, after me. I, I
> am the Lord, and besides me there is no savior" (Is 43:10-11).

John uses the same "I am" statement without a predicate
to convey Christ's pre-existent oneness with the eternal
Godhead in John 6:20; 8:24, 58; 13:19; 18:5, 6, 8. They
imply, however, for John that Jesus, as Word made flesh, is the

ultimate and complete Revealer of what God is like. Only in and through Him can we come to the Father (Jn 14:7).

But to bring this New Testament belief in Jesus Christ as the ultimate communication of God to us and the perfect bestower of God's very inner, Trinitarian life down to specifics, John more often uses the second class of "I am" statements with a predicate or a symbolic term. This is typified by Jesus' statement in our text (Jn 14:6): "I am the way, the truth, and the life."

Similar sayings with a predicate or a symbol are: "I am" . . . the bread of life (Jn 6:35, 48); the living bread (6:51); the bread that has come down from heaven (6:41); the light of the world (8:12; 9:5); the door for the sheep (10:7); the good shepherd (10:11, 14); the resurrection and the life (11:25), and the true vine (15:1, 5).

FAITH IN GOD AND IN JESUS

To BELIEVE that Jesus exists before Abraham was born (Jn 8:59) and that He possesses the same knowledge as His Father, we need the faith that is more than an intellectual assent to a doctrinal statement. We need a faith *in* Him, just as we have faith *in* God. This requires a childlike trust and abandonment without any fear or anxiety to respond completely to God's revelation in Jesus.

John introduces our text, therefore, with the preliminary condition of faith to respond to Jesus as God's way, truth and life. "Do not let your heart be troubled! You have faith in God; have faith in me also" (Jn 14:1). Keeping in mind John's perspective that the historical Jesus is always speaking in this Gospel as the exalted and glorified risen Lord, we hear Jesus calling us to get rid of all fears and worries since He, who is within us, is more powerful than any force outside (1 Jn 4:4), coming from the hostility of the world. There can be, also, no

fear due to Jesus' absence, for He is always with us, dwelling
with the Father and the Spirit inside of us, provided we keep His
words (Jn 14:23).

JESUS, THE WAY

JESUS TELLS us that He goes ahead of us to prepare a place for us
(Jn 14:3). Even though Jesus, the risen Lord, dwells always
within us, yet we are now in exile. The Israelites journeyed in
the desert before they found God's presence in the glorious
Temple built by Solomon on Mt. Zion; yet God had already
pitched His tent among His desert people in the Ark of the
Covenant.

Jesus is our way, the only complete and final way of
reaching our unique "mansion" or place in God's eternal
triune community of love. Each of us is loved uniquely by the
Father in Jesus through His Spirit. Jesus is *the* way for all human
beings. He is the Father's true and only way. All other ways,
such as the Old Testament *Torah* or Law or the various paths of
an enlightening *gnosis* or esoteric knowledge are subsumed
into and fulfilled by Jesus.

Jesus needs no way Himself, for He is the way and the goal
which can never be separated. John's Good News to us is that
now Jesus is the surest, most perfect way to lead us to the Father
without any error or deception, with no hesitation or failing.
Jesus is the *message* and the *medium*. We believe *in* Him. He
has come from the Father and He goes back to the Father. He
possesses the Father's Spirit, in order to lead us to the Father's
home.

God has created us to be "homed" — to use the phrase of
Julian of Norwich of the 14th century — in the Father's love.
We all search desperately for our "home" where we can find
love, peace and joy, security without fear or anxiety. Jesus is the

one who alone can lead us to our eternal home. We have been predestined by the Father from all eternity to "be holy and without blemish in his sight. Out of love he predestined us for himself to become through Jesus Christ his adopted children . . . to the praise of his resplendent grace, with which he has adorned us in his beloved Son" (Ep 1:4-6).

A way is only useful to us if we follow along it to our desired goal. Here we see how our faith is tied to a loving, trustful response in each moment of our human life to follow the way Jesus has opened up for us as He continually opens us up to the values He lived by. Faith, therefore, is a vital and dynamic movement through our union with Jesus. In faith we listen to and obey His Word which becomes a personalized way as we respond in loving surrender and obedience to let Jesus guide us in all things.

PRAYER

1. Jn 14:16
2. Jn 5:19-35
3. Jn 5:36-47
4. Jn 10:22-30
5. Jn 16:25-33
6. 1 Jn 3:19-24

15

"I AM . . . THE TRUTH . . ."
(Jn 14:6)

IN JOHN'S GOSPEL the term *truth* is often used (e.g. Jn 1:14, 17; 3:21; 4:23-24; 5:33; 8:32, 45; 14:6, 17; 16:7, 13; 17:17; 18:37). It is difficult for us to understand exactly what John

88   ENTERING INTO THE HEART OF JESUS

means when he uses this term, especially in our text (Jn 14:6)
that Jesus *is* the truth. Pilate asked Jesus: "What is truth?"
(Jn 18:38). We ask a similar question since we, too, like Pilate,
approach God and Jesus in various ways and hence we understand the term *truth* with different meanings.

We speak truthfully when we do not lie or seek to deceive
anyone by our inner intention or thought. We make a truthful
statement when what we think, state or teach corresponds to an
objective reality and we do not "err," e.g. when we say:
2+2=4. We can be guided by truth when such truth helps us
live in a "correct" way. Finally, we claim some statement or
theory is *true* when it follows logical reasoning or objective,
scientific methods.

But Jesus uses *truth* in a much different way. We might
begin to unravel the Johannine meaning of truth by meditating
on John 8:31-36. Those who accept Jesus with complete certainty as the Divine Word of God, and act upon the contents of
His revelation, will be His disciples and this truth will set them
free. Truth is not something impersonal. It is always relational
and first begins within the triune, divine community of love.

God freely determines to share His Trinitarian life and
happiness with all His human children. God the Father sent His
Son in Jesus Christ to be the human expression, the witness and
revelation of His desire from all eternity to create us and bring
us into *truth* by fulfilling, through Jesus Christ and His Spirit, the
primordial desire in all our hearts to attain meaning and certainty in God's perfect, passionate, self-emptying love for each
of us uniquely.

GOD'S EVERLASTING FIDELITY

THIS SHARING in the complete truth begins through the revealing
and witnessing power of the Holy Spirit who proclaims that

through Jesus Christ we have the same Heavenly Father who unconditionally loves us in the same Spirit of love by which He loves His only begotten Son. We can rely on God's perfect and everlasting fidelity (*emet* in Hebrew) in all His actions, revelations and commands.

God has created us in Jesus Christ to share God's own eternal life. This is truth, and all truthful statements, all logical "truths" flow from and must return to God as the embodiment of all truth. God, therefore, is truthful when, as revealed and witnessed to by the human life of Jesus Christ, God's divine Son, He acts out of His faithful and caring love. But we are set free and become related to the Trinity as we "know" God as *truth* (Jn 8:31-32).

But we are to respond to Jesus' revelation and witness to God's triune, active, truthful fidelity in self-emptying love. Thus we are to "speak the truth in love," as St. Paul exhorts us (Ep 4:15). Only when we "continue in my word," as Jesus says (Jn 8:31), will we become children of the truth.

CHILDLIKE TRUST

THE TEST OF OUR ACCEPTING JESUS as *truth* is measured by what the early Eastern Fathers called *parrhesia*. This is the childlike trust that is grounded through the Spirit of Jesus' revelation — in faith, hope and love — of God's *emet*, or His everlasting fidelity to be always love in action toward His children. This requires that we become "poor in spirit" and this is the first condition for entering into the Kingdom of God (Mt 5:3). It is our condition of realizing, through Jesus' Spirit, that we are held in the Heavenly Father's hands. We can do nothing of ourselves. Yet we rejoice in our weakness and our total dependence upon God our Father.

We abandon ourselves with joy to the care of the Father because we trust completely in His unconditional and faithful love which seeks always and in every situation our complete happiness.

Another word for such poverty of spirit is *humility*. It is always connected with truth — God's fidelity to love us with self-emptying love. But until Jesus — God's Word become flesh — emptied Himself in His death on the cross for love of us, the fullness of God's *truth* could not have been revealed.

This is the pivotal message in John's Gospel. God's truth is encountered by us in Jesus: ". . . grace and *truth* have come through Jesus Christ" (Jn 1:17).

PRAYER

1. Jn 8:31-36	3. Jn 16:5-15	5. Ep 4:23-32
2. Jn 18:33-38	4. Jn 17:15-19	6. Ep 1:3-14

16

"I AM . . . THE LIFE"
(Jn 14:6)

ALL FOUR EVANGELISTS treat of the life and death of our Lord. We can discover in each of their Gospels a distinct unifying theme around which aspects of the inexhaustible personality of Christ are presented to us. Even a cursory reading of St. John's Gospel and the other Johannine writings will reveal that his central theme is *life*. Jesus Christ is the *Life* of the world.

While the Synoptic writers use this term in reference to Christ only 16 times, John uses it in his Gospel alone 36 times. The Synoptic writers, on the contrary, present Christ and His mission on this earth under the image of the kingdom of God, using this phrase 82 times, while John uses it only once. St. John Chrysostom indicates the reason commenting upon John's Gospel:

> Christ makes mention so often of life because life is one of the things most ardently desired by men and there is nothing more pleasant than the thought of never dying.

Christ describes Himself as *life*: "I am the resurrection and the life" (Jn 11:25). But John is less interested in presenting Jesus Christ as subsistent life, whose nature is to be absolute, uncaused life (which, of course, He is), than he is in showing Him as the giver of this life to the world, a life that the world does not otherwise possess, except through Christ.

In the First Epistle John calls Christ the "Word who is life and who imparts it" (1 Jn 1:2). "This Life has manifested Himself" (ibid.). He has revealed Himself in order that we might share in His life. "I have come that they may have life and have it in abundance" (Jn 10:10). In Him is the life (Jn 1:4), and no one can have this life except through Jesus Christ.

SEMITIC CONCEPT OF LIFE

YET JOHN COMPREHENDS the notion of life according to the traditional Semitic concept, developed over centuries of speculation before the Incarnation. John incorporates this into his understanding of Christ's relationship to the human world.

Upon this understanding he creates his original point of emphasis.

In the Old Testament we find a very gradual development of the idea of life, culminating a few centuries before Christ in a full idea of an eternal life, of immortality with God. In the rudimentary notion, *life* was conceived as the greatest gift given by God. "All that man possesses, he abandons in order to save his life" (Jb 2:4). Those consigned to Sheol still have existence, but no life; thus life must be more than simple existence. Yahweh is the God of the living, the living God, the Source of all life. He gives life and takes it away. The Jew prayed to God in the words of the Psalmist: "Thou wilt not leave my soul in the place of death, or allow thy faithful servant to see corruption. Thou wilt show me the way of life, make me full of gladness in thy presence" (Ps 15:10-11).

Thus, life is the greatest of goods to be desired and possessed. To the just, God promises a long, full life; to the wicked, a premature death. But it is only in the second century before Christ's coming that a clear idea of an eternal life after death emerges in the Jewish tradition. Temporal life is considered a testing period for the life to come. But the future life is considered a continuation of this present life, free of everything painful, like death, injustice and suffering.

CHRISTIAN CONCEPT OF LIFE

THE CHRISTIAN ERA BUILT upon this Semitic tradition. The Christian writers were convinced, as was John, that "theology of life" was an accurate Semitic description of Christ's message. Thus we see strong Semitic influences in the idea of salvation conceived as new life, with Christ as the life-giver and faith as the seed or germ of life. The sacraments are considered as carriers of this divine life which is fostered through asceticism or purification of the obstacles to further growth and virtuous living.

But such writers also saw in the New Testament the Jewish concept of a future life that stressed it in its eschatological literalness. The present life is conceived, not as the same life, but as a distinct period of probation. The moral aspects of this present life are stressed as important only in view of the future, eternal life.

One of John's original contributions is that he builds around the Semitic eschatological hope of a future, eternal life the dynamic concept of life that is here and now eternal. This new, paradoxical life admits of degrees of development, as does all life, but John's striking insight is that it is *already* eternal life. Keeping to the primitive Semitic concept of life as the attainment of complete health, joy and happiness, John emphasizes the continuity between this present life in Christ and our future life after death. There is no clash between "natural" and "supernatural" because for John there is only one life, the eternal life of God already lived by Christians in this earthly existence. The manner of enjoying this life now differs from that of the future life, but the life itself is one and the same; it is continuous with the life already possessed, but it is also a life that admits of varying levels of growth in oneness with the very triune life of God.

We are already children of God (1 Jn 3:1); but we do not know what awaits us in the life to come. Sharing in God's life means coming to "know" God experientially in a similar way that the Father knows the Son through the Spirit who manifests this life through mutual relationships of loving self-surrender between the Father and the Son. "And this is the sum of eternal life — their knowing you, the only true God, and your ambassador Jesus Christ" (Jn 17:3). It is Jesus' prime goal in His earthly existence to reveal and make possible, through His Holy Spirit, the triune life which His Father has decreed from all eternity

to share with us human beings by sending us His only Son
(Jn 3:16).

LIFE — A PRESENT REALITY

THE CENTRAL PURPOSE of John's Gospel is to foster a deeper faith
among Christians "that Jesus is the Messiah, the Son of God,
and that, through your belief, you may have life in his name"
(Jn 20:31). This life is to be possessed *now*. It comes to us by
hearing the Word and believing in Him through our complete
response in obedience to His commands. Faith in Christ allows
us to pass, even now, from eschatological death, the death of
God's life in us, to His life (cf. Jn 5:24-25).

John similarly teaches the *now* possession of eternal life in
his First Epistle:

> We know that we have passed from death to life, because we love
> our brothers. He who does not love abides in death. Everyone who
> hates his brothers is a murderer, and you know that no murderer has
> eternal life abiding in him (1 Jn 3:14-15).

John often simply drops out the adjective, *eternal*, when he
speaks of this present life in Christ. "He who believes in the Son
possesses life" (Jn 3:36; 6:40-47). "He who eats of my flesh
and drinks of my blood has eternal life" (Jn 6:54). There is only
one life that is the healthy, full life of a human person, and that
is to live the same life that one should live eternally in the life of
the Trinity (Jn 17:3).

PRAYER

1. Jn 6:35-58   3. Jn 11:20-44   5. 1 Jn 5:1-12
2. Jn 5:24-25   4. Jn 1:1-18   6. 1 Cor 15:42-57

17

"HE WHO SEES
ME SEES THE FATHER" (Jn 14:9)

TRUE RELIGION should have as its purpose the satisfying of the universal, yearning desire within the heart of each human being to move out of "unreality" into the world of God's reality, out of a shadowy, darkened existence of selfishness into one of enlightenment and meaningfulness. Religions should prepare the individual to discover the meaning of all reality in an intimate union with God as the Source of all love and meaningfulness.

Christianity is a religion that leads its faithful in a commitment to a person, Jesus Christ. Hinduism and Buddhism teach a way or path to enlightenment. Gautama Buddha is important for Buddhists because of his teachings. For them the historical details of his life are not important. Whether he rose from the dead or not is unimportant. What is important is how to reach his level of enlightenment and so attain the *Buddha* state of everlasting bliss.

To be Christian, however, is to put one's whole life in a faithful and loving obedience to Jesus Christ. He did live humanly as did Gautama Buddha. He was enlightened, but He also rose from the dead and now He lives as our Life. Christian faith means that Jesus Christ now lives within us and shares with us, through the release of His Holy Spirit, His Life everlasting.

It is by faith given us as a gift from the Spirit of the risen Christ that we *know* in a manner beyond all rational knowledge and wisdom that the historical Jesus of Nazareth is truly the incarnate Word of God, bringing us eternal life.

> Something which has existed since the beginning,
> that we have heard,
> and we have seen with our own eyes,
> that we have watched
> and touched with our hands:
> the Word, who is life —
> this is our subject.
> That life was made visible:
> we saw it and we are giving our testimony,
> telling you of the eternal life
> which was with the Father and has been made visible to us.
> What we have seen and heard
> we are telling you
> so that you too may be in union with us,
> as we are in union
> with the Father
> and with his Son Jesus Christ.
> We are writing this to you to make our own joy complete (1 Jn 1:1-14).

A COMMITMENT OF LOVE

WE ACCEPT IN FAITH the faith experience of the first Christian community that bears witness to Jesus' transforming power over His followers, molding them into a sharing community of people who love one another as He loved them (Jn 15:12).

Such a faith in the risen Lord as one who is in the midst of Christians assembled as members of His Body, the Church, is an absurdity according to the "wisdom" of the *world* (1 Cor 2:7-9). Belief in Jesus risen cannot be so much a fact that is proved historically. It is belief that calls for a response in love as the Spirit of the risen Lord continually reveals the living Christ within the heart of each believer. Such an ongoing experience in sharing the "new life" of Jesus Christ in the context of our everyday life fills us with excitement. We respond with joy and peace as we move continually from life to Life. Death and sin are being destroyed as we experience in the "sacrament of the present moment" the burning love of God almighty, three Persons in a oneness of love for us as individuals and as members of the total Christ.

"LET US SEE THE FATHER"

IN OUR TEXT the apostle Philip utters the plea to Jesus: "Master let us see the Father, and we shall be satisfied" (Jn 14:8-9). Jesus responds to Philip's request with a question that hints at impatience on Jesus' part with the slowness of Philip, the other apostles and Christians in the post-Easter community. "Philip, so long a time have I been in your midst, and you do not know me? He who sees me sees the Father. How, then, can you say: 'Let us see the Father'? Do you not believe that I am in the Father and the Father is in me? . . . Believe me, all of you, when I say that I am in the Father and the Father is in me; but if not, at least believe on the strength of what I am doing" (14:9-11).

Philip represents all "religious" persons who consider Jesus as a mere teacher of true statements that might lead an individual into a mystical knowledge of God through such an objective teaching or kind of dogma or ritual. The teacher would be dispensable. Jesus would merely pass on, in a magical way, a formula whereby one would be "saved" and find full meaningfulness to have all desires fulfilled in what could be considered as complete happiness "in Heaven." Such a person finds it difficult to understand a true and *faithful* encounter with the community of God's love through a process of living in a relationship with the indwelling Trinity by faith, in hope and with love.

It is the difference between religions that give the "faith-ful" a knowledge "about God," a *gnosis* that does not trans-form the whole person but only touches the intellect, and those that lead a person into living faithful encounters with God as community of love in the mystery of faith.

Jesus is telling us as He responds to Philip's request that there is no other way to see the Father than to take a good look at Jesus in faith — believing. No one can see the full face of the Heavenly Father. Moses, like Philip, pleaded of God to let him see His face (Ex 33:18). Yahweh answered: "You cannot see my face, for man cannot see me and live" (Ex 33:20-21).

John's Gospel continues this "apophatic" approach, stressing God's holiness, awesomeness and complete tran-scendence (Jn 1:18; 6:46; cf. 1 Jn 4:12). Yet John builds a Christology around this pivotal revelation of Christianity. Christianity is unique among all other religions because it stresses that this historical person, Jesus Christ, is truly God, as well as man. He is the medium of God's revelation: "I am the way" (Jn 14:6); but He also is the message.

THE GOOD NEWS

THE "GOOD NEWS" of Christianity is that now all human beings can see God's "face" by looking into the face of Jesus of the Gospels. "Seeing" God in Jesus is not a physical seeing. Seeing, in John's statement, is an ongoing process of faithful response to Jesus' indwelling presence as risen Lord, as the Son of God, as one who is not only with God, but *is* God! (Jn 1:1).

He is the perfect image of the unseen God (Col 1:15). He reveals or "unveils" for us that God is like Jesus. He acts as Jesus acts. His values and judgments are exactly as Jesus preached and acted upon. God's love is perfectly manifested in Jesus' words and activities, but, above all, in His being the single, only begotten Word made flesh who emptied Himself for love of us in death on the cross.

The suffering Servant of Yahweh, lifted up on the cross, will draw (Jn 12:32) to Himself — and, therefore, to true and ultimate meaningfulness — those who believe He is truly God. Only those converted, who have become like little children, will be able to see by faith that the Father lives as Jesus lives, that Jesus dies out of love for each of us and His very love is the same love the Father has for us, namely, the very same Holy Spirit.

"I AND THE FATHER ARE ONE"

JOHN GIVES HIS TYPICAL FORMULA of "reciprocal immanence" as the reason why whoever believes in Jesus can see the Father. "I am in the Father and the Father is in me" (Jn 14:10). Here is John's fundamental teaching of the indwelling Trinity. God is one in many, a loving community of an *I-Thou* in a *We-community* of love.

The personhood of the Son is realized only in the self-emptying gift of the Father in the hidden, bonding love of the Holy Spirit. The Father finds His uniqueness as Father in Jesus Christ, His only begotten Son, again in the unifying love of the Spirit. Jesus in His high-priestly prayer to the Father would pray, before His death and after His glorification, that His prayer would be everlasting and efficacious: "The glory you have bestowed on me I have bestowed on them, that they may be one as we are one, I in them and you in me. Thus their oneness will be perfected. The world must come to acknowledge that I am your ambassador, and that you love them as you love me" (Jn 17:22-23).

Such a statement of indwelling reciprocity is not a clear and distinct idea of speculative theology, easily comprehended by human intellection. God's Spirit gives such experiential knowledge by faith to those who respond to Jesus as God's living Word made flesh. It is a statement of living relationships, of encounters in faith and love through self-surrender, that becomes a transforming experience in which one comes to know Jesus as "the way, the truth and the life" (Jn 14:6).

"HE WILL DO
EVEN GREATER THINGS THAN I DO"

THE RESULT of encountering Jesus through faith as the one who gives the fullest meaning and happiness to our lives empowers us to "do the things I am doing; in fact, he will do even greater things than I do" (Jn 14:12).

What are the "things" Jesus does? Jesus saves. He does this through His preachings, healings and miracles. He promises to all His followers who believe in Him, that they, too, will do similar "things," works which will serve as an incarnational continuation and completion of Christ's revelatory activity.

Although Jesus "is going home to the Father" (Jn 14:13), His disciples can ask anything in His name and He will do it (14:14). The basic reason is that Jesus' "going home to the Father" is not to be conceived in a spatial way. Jesus' *going* does not separate the disciples from Him, but, in a new presence as glorified by the Father and able to live in His followers, Jesus returns and brings them into the Source of all reality, the indwelling Trinity, Father, Son and Holy Spirit.

The "greater works" are to be seen as Jesus carrying on His mission after His resurrection through the outpouring of the Holy Spirit in and through the Church-community. Now the

Trinity, dwelling in the individual Christian and in the Christian community that lives by faith, hope and love, will empower them to extend the works of Jesus.

These works will be "greater" since they are still His work being brought to greater completion throughout the entire world in a way that the historical Jesus in His limitations in space and time never could have accomplished. We, as His members, can never put limits to our faith and prayer, since it is Jesus in His Father's Spirit of love who continues to work in His members.

We can dare to do greater things than Jesus did, only because in His resurrectional life He calls us to be His hands and feet, His lips and eyes, and to extend His salvation to the whole world. St. Paul beautifully summarizes this exciting truth of John's Gospel:

> Even though we once valued Christ by what he was externally, we now value him by this standard no longer. If, then, any man is in Christ, he is a new creation; the old state of things has gone; wonderful to tell, it has been made over, absolutely new! All this comes from the action of God, who has reconciled us to himself through Christ, and has entrusted us with this ministry of reconciliation. We know that God was truly reconciling the world to himself in Christ, not reckoning against men their sins, and entrusting to us the message of reconciliation.
>
> We are, therefore, Christ's ambassadors; we know that God makes appeal through us. We beg you, for the sake of Christ, to be reconciled to God (2 Cor 5:16-21).

PRAYER

1. Jn 14:6-15	3. Jn 17:4-19	5. 2 Cor 5:16-21
2. Jn 16:5-15	4. 1 Jn 5:1-12	6. Ep 4:1-16

18

"HE WILL GRANT
YOU ANOTHER ADVOCATE" (Jn 14:16)

THE FUNDAMENTAL QUESTION of all religions is how can we know what God is like and how can we be transformed by surrendering to God's power and gentle love? Christianity, especially as seen in the four Gospels, presents Jesus Christ as holding primary place in revealing to the human race the invisible Godhead. He is the bridge from material creation that leads us into the heart of God.

He is the communicating Word of God in and through His historical human existence. Who sees Him sees the Father (Jn 14:9). To the person who hears His word and keeps it He and the Father will come and dwell within in a permanent manner of indwelling union (14:23).

Jesus is God's "advocate" or *paraclete*. Specifically He "stands up" for us, interceding to "save" us. He is our helper, consoler, counselor. Yet in order to accept the historical Jesus as one who died and was raised by the Father as exalted in glory and given by the Father all power, the Christian writers, especially John the Evangelist, highlight the importance of the sending of the Holy Spirit.

THE SPIRIT AND THE RISEN JESUS

JOHN DOES NOT WISH to imply that Jesus leaves us and the Spirit takes His place. He does not mean that one advocate, namely,

Jesus, leaves our historical world and the Holy Spirit replaces Him as the advocate among us in our historical time and place. When in John's Gospel Jesus promises to give us "another Advocate" (Jn 14:16), we perhaps should translate the word, *Paraclete*, in this text as "Supporter" or "Helper."

In Johannine and Pauline theology the Holy Spirit does not replace the earthly presence of Jesus exalted. The Spirit makes the risen Jesus present and actively involved as the one who is among His followers in the community of love. The Spirit more fully "unveils" the primary revelation of God's Trinitarian community of love to those who keep the commandments (or words) of Jesus (Jn 14:25-26; 14:23).

THE WORKING OF THE HOLY SPIRIT

WHEREVER THE SPIRIT OPERATES in the Old and New Testaments, He operates as the agent or force of God's power. The Spirit is the creative force of God moving toward chaos and darkness and death and drawing the "void" into a sharing of God's being (Gn 1:2). The Spirit is a powerful wind stirring stillness into a dynamic new life. He is the one who gives new hearts (Ezk 36:26), anointing kings, judges and prophets with wisdom and knowledge. Jesus receives the Spirit as a power, enabling Him to preach, teach, heal and perform miracles.

In His death-resurrection Jesus is raised up by the Spirit into the fullness of power. "Yes, but he was crucified through weakness, and still he lives now through the power of God" (2 Cor 13:4). The power is the Spirit, but He imparts its fullness to the risen Lord who shares it now with us. "All power is given to me. . . . Going therefore, teach you all nations" (Mt 28:18-19).

THE GIFT OF THE HOLY SPIRIT

IN OUR TEXT JESUS PROMISES His disciples that He "will ask the Father, and he will grant you another Advocate to be with you for all time to come, the Spirit of Truth!" (Jn 14:16-17). The Father will send Jesus' followers His Spirit (Jn 14:16; Mk 15:26; Lk 11:13). But Jesus also will send the Spirit as the one proceeding not only from the Father but from the Son (Jn 14:26; 16:14). The Spirit within the Trinity is the mutual bond of unity between the Father and the Son. The same "actions" of the Spirit, within the Trinity, go on in our historical world through the death-resurrection of Jesus Christ.

To the risen Christ, it has been given to bestow upon us the power and glory of God's Spirit. We share in the gift of Christ's Spirit in varying degrees. Yet Christ pours out the fullness since He Himself has received of that fullness (Col 2:9-10). The Spirit is Gift, dependent upon God's free choice, since He is God's Love, freely creating us and gifting us with a sharing, a participation (2 P 1:4) in God's very own community of love, the Trinity.

The Spirit forms the whole Christ, in the sense of His mystical body and not only individual human persons who relate exclusively and vertically to God. As we share in the one Spirit, eternally poured out in Christ, we can see that there can be no sharing in Christ's resurrection and His glory without the Spirit of love. It is the Spirit who raises us to a new creation in Christ. It is the Spirit who quickens us through faith, hope and love that we might live ever more consciously in our oneness in Christ.

In and through the Holy Spirit we become aware that we and Christ are the recipients of the one, same, vivifying action of the Holy Spirit. Now we, too, can share in the properties of God's Spirit as the risen Jesus does. As the body of the risen

Jesus is spiritualized by the Spirit, so also, but not in the fullness yet, are our bodies holy temples of God in whom resides the Holy Spirit (1 Cor 3:16; 6:19).

THE SPIRIT BRINGS US FREEDOM

THUS THE INDWELLING SPIRIT CATCHES us up in an ongoing process of our becoming God's children through His regeneration which allows us to be "born of the Spirit" (Jn 3:6). The light of the Spirit leads us out of all darkness and illusion. We are gradually enlightened by His indwelling presence to know the truth that we are in Christ, even now sharing in the life of His risen Body. This same Spirit brings us into a sharing of Christ's resurrection by revealing to us that the same Jesus who died for love of us still loves us with that infinity of love reached on the cross when He passed from death to resurrection (cf. Gal 2:20).

As we yield to such a dynamic love of the present risen Jesus, we experience a new freedom of being children of God, loved immensely by God Himself. Fears and anxieties are shed as we experience new powers to love, to be "toward" God, ourselves and our neighbors. We experience a sharing in Christ's cosmic oneness with the entire material universe, which brings about a kind of eucharistic sharing as we are touched and molded into the Body of the risen Christ.

Freed from sin by the indwelling Spirit of the risen Lord, we no longer live in darkness nor do we want to. "No one who has been begotten by God sins; because God's seed remains inside him, he cannot sin when he has been begotten by God" (1 Jn 3:9). As the Spirit constantly reveals to us from within our true identity as children loved infinitely by a perfect Father through Jesus Christ who has died for us, we can live each

moment in Him and with Him. We can learn to accept our true
identity as fully mature children of God, as Jesus did.

RECEIVING
THE SPIRIT IN THE NOW-MOMENT

BUT THIS TAKES PLACE only in the present *now* of God's love for
us in Christ Jesus. The Holy Spirit progressively brings about
our regeneration as children of God to the degree that we yield
to His illuminations and inspirations. These give us the conviction that we possess an inner dignity as children of God, united
with the risen Christ, a part of His very Body.

Paul is one with John's teaching on the discernment of
Christ's Spirit of Truth when he writes: "If you are guided by the
Spirit you will be in no danger of yielding to self-indulgence . . .
the Spirit is totally against the flesh. . . . What the Spirit brings is
very different: love, joy, peace, patience, kindness, goodness,
trustfulness, gentleness and self-control" (Gal 5:16, 18, 22).

LOVE EVERYONE

THROUGH THE GIFT OF FAITH, we come to believe in God's
unconditional outpoured love for us in Jesus Christ. As we
believe and live in union with the indwelling Trinity, Father,
Son and Holy Spirit, we come to believe in God's unconditional love for all persons and for the entirety of His created
world.

John the Evangelist stresses the connection between our
faith and love for Jesus and our keeping His commandments.
"He who accepts my commandments and treasures them — he

is the one that loves me. And he that loves me will, in turn, be loved by my Father; and I will love him, and will manifest myself to him" (Jn 14:21).

So much of Johannine spirituality emphasizes the *praxis* or practical living out of the *truth* revealed by Jesus Christ in the context of our daily lives. Christ's revealed message is reduced by John to the ever-recurring theme put simply: If you love Me, keep My commandments. These are My commandments: that you love My Father and Me in Our Spirit of love and — in the same Spirit that My Father and I will always send you — you must love one another as I love you (Jn 15:12, 17).

One becomes a Christian through the power of the Holy Spirit in a process of keeping the commandments of love for God and neighbor by actively helping others wherever needed. The Spirit reveals that God lives in such a self-emptying love within the Trinitarian community. Such a divine loving community transforms us into a loving community in oneness with Christ. This is the work of the Spirit: "We exercise mutual love because he first loved us. If anyone says, 'I love God,' yet hates his brother, he is a liar. Why? Because he who does not love his brother whom he sees, cannot love God whom he does not see. Besides, we have received this commandment from God: He who loves God must love his brother also" (1 Jn 4:20-21).

PRAYER

1. Jn 14:16-31   3. Jn 16:5-15   5. 1 Jn 4:7-21
2. Jn 15:9-17   4. Jn 17:20-26   6. Jm 2:14-26

19

" I AM THE VINE,
YOU ARE THE BRANCHES" (Jn 15:5)

CHRISTIANITY IS A RELIGION that builds a loving community, modeled on and empowered by the very intimate, loving, self-sacrificing community of the Trinity, Father, Son and Holy Spirit. It is rooted in God who wishes to communicate Himself to us in the most intimate of unions. Holy Scripture often uses the image of husband and wife to describe this tender relationship between God and ourselves. And we are to love one another as God — through Jesus — loves us in the Holy Spirit.

In His second farewell discourse in John's Gospel Jesus uses the parabolic discourse of the vine and the branches to convey, not only this great, intimate union between us individually with the indwelling Trinity, but also our self-giving, through the power of the risen Jesus, to others within the community of love, the Church. He teaches the necessity of our being united with Him if we are to reach human fulfillment. He insists that this fulfillment is to be measured by the love we have for others as we serve to build up the community of love, the total Christ, the Body and Head, the New Israel.

VINE / VINEYARD
HISTORY IN SCRIPTURE

THE AGRICULTURAL IMAGE which Jesus uses meant much to His listeners in Palestine, and it had a long religious significance in the history of the Jewish people. The Prophet Isaiah spoke of Israel as a vineyard planted by God with great effort, "but sour grapes were all that it gave" (Is 5:2). God's word is even stronger through the Prophet Jeremiah: "How is it you have become a degenerate plant, you bastard vine?" (Jr 2:21). God spoke of the vine branches as useless and "fit only for burning," to use the words of the Prophet Ezekiel (Ezk 15:6). Thus the vine was a symbol for Israel in the thinking of the Jews at the time of our Lord.

John builds upon the Old Testament and the Synoptic writings (Mk 12:1-12) to make Jesus the image of the true and only real vine. He alone is the way, truth and life (Jn 14:6). He replaces in His person the Temple and all its cultic practices of worship. Now the Christian community, one with Christ who feeds the members to become a new "creation," becomes the "place" where true praise and worship and pleasure are given to God. Christ is the center of John's teaching. Jesus as the Son of God is the sole revealer now who is the message, but also the medium, who as its center brings about a community of worship and praise.

JESUS — THE TRUE VINE

JESUS IS THE ROOT that gives vitality to all the branches.

> I am the true vine, you are the branches.
> Make your home in me, as I make mine in you.
> As a branch cannot bear fruit all by itself,
> but must remain part of the vine,
> neither can you unless you remain in me.
> I am the vine,
> you are the branches.

Whoever remains in me, with me in him,
bears fruit in plenty;
for cut off from me you can do nothing.
Anyone who does not remain in me
is like a branch that has been thrown away
and withers;
these branches are collected and thrown on the fire,
and they are burnt (Jn 15:1, 4-6).

PRUNING OF THE BRANCHES

JESUS INSISTS not only on our union with Him, but also on the necessity that, as branches, we must be pruned by His Father, the Vinedresser, if we are to bring forth more fruit. Two activities are suggested as being works of the Vinedresser. The Father prunes away branches that are unfruitful and He trims or purifies the fruitful branches in order that they might bear more abundant fruit (Jn 15:1-3).

Jesus tells us that there are some branches that bear no fruit. They merely drain the vine of its energy. These are to be pruned away and burned. No doubt in this allegory Jesus was referring to the Jews who heard His words but bore no fruit in building a loving community of the people of God. But He also must have had in mind His future followers who would profess to be Christians and yet would never bring forth deeds of Christian love. These would also include the apostates down through the centuries who would refuse to listen to the teachings of Jesus given within His Body, the Church. He is saying that unless those who have heard His words put them into practice with life-giving deeds of love, they will be fruitless branches fit only to be pruned away, cut off as such from Christ, the Vine, who alone brings forth true life and fruit that will last forever.

But He tells us also that the Heavenly Father, out of love for His children, prunes those Christians who are already alive in Christ. His motive is to enable them to bring forth greater fruit. Such pruning is therapy unto greater life. Jesus gives us an example in His own earthly life. He was constantly in union with the Father, yet the Father pruned Him of all excessive baggage, of any self-centeredness in order to equip Him for His great work of bringing salvation to the world. "For the Lord trains the ones that he loves and he punishes all those that he acknowledges as his sons. Suffering is part of your training: God is treating you as his sons" (Heb 12:6-7).

ABIDING IN CHRIST

TRUE CHRISTIANS ARE those who live consciously through faith, hope and love in the union with Christ as the guiding force. They are called to abide in Him. No matter how weak they are, when they are aware of such a friend, the Bridegroom, loving them passionately as His very own Bride, they are given the ability to accomplish infinitely more than what they could ever do alone: ". . . for cut off from me, you can do nothing" (Jn 15:5).

This is the incredibly good news John presents to us. The Vine exists even without the branches. But the branches cannot be true, living branches unless they are receiving life through sap from the vine. God pours into our hearts His love through the Spirit whom He gives us (Rm 5:5) and who dwells within us (Rm 8:9), in order that in His Spirit we might know that we are really children of God (1 Jn 3:1), made heirs with Christ of Heaven forever (Rm 8:17). Jesus is the way, the truth and the life who leads us into the most intimate presence of the triune God who wishes effectively to come and abide within us, Father, Son and Spirit (Jn 14:23).

We praise God most when we live consciously in Christ in order that with His mind we may glorify the Father in His Spirit of love. We seek always to please the Father as Jesus did (Jn 13:31-32). Whatever we pray for, it will be granted when we strive always to glorify the Father (15:17).

The work of the risen Jesus is to release His Spirit who divinizes us, "regenerates" us, making us beautiful and "alluring" to Christ, the Bridegroom. It is in the "heart," scriptural language for the innermost core of one's being, that we discover our true self in the oneness we enjoy with Christ. He inebriates us with the beauty of His divine-human person. In our heart He meets us in an *I-Thou* relationship. Through His Spirit we understand that, just as the Father loves Jesus, so Jesus loves us (Jn 15:9). He, God-Man, has died for us. That love for each one of us hurled Him into a new, resurrectional life which He now at each moment wishes to share with us.

We enter into this intimacy alone with Christ. Only individually, in deep prayer, can we realize through the Spirit that Jesus' *kenotic* or self-emptying love for us on the cross is the image of the same love the Father and the Holy Spirit share with Him on our behalf. Jesus the Bridegroom continually addresses us in the beautiful words of the Song of Songs: "How beautiful you are, my Beloved, and how delightful!" (Sg 1:16). By Christ's Spirit, we "ravish" the heart of Christ. We know that His love, His Spirit, has transformed us into persons capable of affecting the heart of Jesus. He ardently and passionately desires to be more united with us. Through the humility of the Trinity, God freely seeks our love in return. The flame of God's love for us is sent by the Father and the Son as a sharing in the Spirit who is love.

The greatest happiness you and I can possess is to become increasingly aware of the burning love of the Trinity dwelling within us at all times and to seek to return this flame of love to the triune indwelling God. No obstacle can overcome the force of such a burning love that God has for us. No waters can extinguish this flaming fire of love that Christ has for us.

LOVE ONE ANOTHER

WE HAVE BEEN SWEPT UP into the marital union with Christ so that we now habitually experience His loving presence power-fully and peacefully at the core of our very being. This presence moves out of us, but takes us along, in loving service to the world around us. In other human beings we find the same Christ, laughing in the joyful, and suffering in those who are heavy-burdened. In great love and responsibility, we are drawn to serve our neighbor with an active love that will smooth away lines of fear, grief and consternation on the faces of those who suffer. And the quality of our intimacy with Christ and our transformation by His love through His Spirit are to be measured by our keeping Christ's commandment: "Love one another as I love you. No one can give a greater proof of his love than by laying down his life for his friends. . . . This is all I command you: love one another" (Jn 15:12-17). As we look into the eyes of each person that we are privileged to en-counter, all walls of separation tumble as by our look we proclaim: "I am your brother. I love you! You are beautiful in God's love. How can I serve you to make you discover the beauty that I see in you by faith and hope?"

QUALITIES OF TRUE LOVE

SUCH LOVE IS A DYING to our own narcissism or self-love. It is a finding of our true self in serving others. In giving, we receive; yet we seek only to give. We put no price tag on our loving service. St. Paul characterizes what the true fruit of love is. We may well possess great gifts of prophecy, of understanding all mysteries, of knowing all knowledge, of faith so strong it could move mountains; we could give millions of dollars to the poor, and even surrender our body to be burned, but if we have not true love, our other talents and good works are of no value.

> Love is always patient and kind; it is never jealous; love is never boastful or conceited; it is never rude or selfish; it does not take offense, and is not resentful. Love takes no pleasure in other people's sins but delights in the truth; it is always ready to excuse, to trust, to hope, and to endure whatever comes (1 Cor 13:4-7).

By remaining in intimate union with the indwelling Jesus, we can bring forth such love. We can experience that we *are* love toward all whom we meet. This is the purpose of our life: to become godly with the very God-life within us expressed through love toward others. This is possible only by being a conscious branch inserted into the Vine that is Jesus Christ. We are called to bring forth Jesus in this world. He needs our hands and feet, our mind, lips and talents in order that He can unite the world to Himself. Yet we need to realize that we are already one with Him. His life lives within us who believe. We are truly branches receiving at every moment the life-giving energy from the Vine that is Christ. The divine Vine sends His life coursing through our entire being in our oneness with and in Him. We go forth to build a similar community of love to the degree that we consciously have allowed ourselves to be *"inserted"* into the True Vine.

PRAYER

Instead of the usual scriptural texts offered for individual prayer, let me suggest the following meditation on our chosen text of the vine and the branches.

After relaxing on body, soul and spirit levels, breathe gently and deeply in and hear Jesus say: "I the Vine." Breathe out as Jesus says: "You the branches." Experience His life flowing through every part and member of your being. Know that this union endures as long as you, the branch, are tied irrevocably to Him through your effective desire to surrender and obey His commands. In this life shared with Jesus you can bring forth much fruit in loving service for others, as Jesus loved the persons He met in His lifetime.

20

"...AS THE FATHER LOVES ME, SO I LOVE YOU" (Jn 15:9)

FOR ME THESE WORDS ARE the most significant, the most revealing of Jesus Christ's mission on earth. St. Athanasius succinctly summarizes the purpose of the Incarnation in these words:

> The Divine Word was made man that we might become gods. He was made visible through His body in order that we might have an idea of the invisible Father. He has supported the outrages of men in order that we might have a part of His immortality (*De Incarnatione Verbi*).

This is the incredibly good news Jesus has come to reveal to us. "He who sees me sees the Father" (Jn 14:9). There can be no other way in God's historical revelation whereby we can truly be certain of the Father's infinite love for us than what His Spirit reveals to us in and through the message and the very medium of Jesus Christ. He is the very message of God's love for us, given to us through the medium of His divine-human person.

As the Heavenly Father eternally begets His Son, so in the economy of history, in the life of Jesus Christ and in a parallel way in our own lives, that same Father is begetting His Son, Jesus Christ, and through Him and His Holy Spirit, He is also begetting us in His Son to be His very own children. "See what kind of love the Father has bestowed on us that we should be children not merely in name but in reality" (1 Jn 3:1).

St. Cyril of Alexandria writes:

> By the Incarnation we also in Him and through Him according to nature and grace have been made sons of God. According to nature insofar as we are one in Him (through the same human nature); by participation and according to grace through Himself in the Spirit (*Ad Theodosium*).

The end of our Christian lives is to grow continually into an ever-increasing awareness of our oneness in Christ Jesus. This is what the Greek Fathers call *divinization*. We are to live in the "likeness" of Jesus Christ, that is, to share in His very own life made possible by the Holy Spirit. St. Bernard preached that God entices us to love Him by attracting us to the humanity of His Son. Jesus Christ images the divinity of God which radiates through the frailty and lowliness of His humanity. His meekness and gentleness draw us to surrender, without any threatening fear, to His Spirit. The power and glory of God in His Word radiates in the teachings, miracles and healings of Jesus in Scripture.

It is through this man, Jesus of Nazareth, who will die and be raised up from the dead, that all of God's grace and truth will come to us.

> Indeed, from his fullness we have, all of us, received — yes, grace in return for grace, . . . grace and truth have come through Jesus Christ. No one has ever seen God; it is the only Son, who is nearest to the Father's heart, who has made him known (Jn 1:16-18).

Jesus Christ perfectly and faithfully represents His Father to us in the human communication of words and actions. When He loves us, especially by emptying Himself on the cross unto the last drop of water and blood, we can have absolute certitude that this is the way the Father loves each of us. Everything He says or does is *the* Word of God. He can do nothing but what the Father tells Him to do. Yet only Jesus Christ, the second Person of the Trinity, in His human nature goes to His death. It is not the Father who dies for us nor the Holy Spirit. Yet all three Persons are involved in the incarnation and redemption, and in our sanctification, each according to His own personalized acts.

The Father begets His Son through the overshadowing of the Spirit, as St. Luke records (Lk 1:35). The Father continues in His personal role as Begetter in our own divinization through His Son and the Holy Spirit. We can say that the Father loves us as He loves His Son, for their love is the Holy Spirit. Yet we receive the Father and the Son's love of the Spirit according to the potential God has placed in each of us to grow in the likeness of Jesus Christ, God-Man. We remain always human beings, yet we are made participators of God's very own nature (2 P 1:4).

GOD WITHIN US

As WE PROGRESS in deeper prayer, we grow more intimately in union with God as Trinity, the core of all reality, and we begin to live in the power of that burning love which surrounds us in all things and permeates the depths of our being. Prayer moves away from a *doing* act — above all from a speaking *to* God as to an object — to become a constant state of *being* in His love.

If Jesus loves us as the Father loves Him, how did the human Jesus experience this burning love of the Father for

Himself? Prayer, for Jesus, was adjusting His whole being to the presence of the Father and the Spirit dwelling within His humanity. It was surrendering in His human consciousness to the Trinitarian God, the Father, Son and Holy Spirit. To pray was for Jesus to be receptive to God's personalized love at every moment. He surrendered to that love and lived it.

As Jesus grew in wisdom and knowledge and grace before God and men (Lk 2:52), He entered into a fuller human awareness of the Father's perfect love and self-giving. For us, contemplation is a growth through the infusion of faith, hope and love by the Spirit of Jesus Christ. We grow in awareness that God is always present, whom we contemplate by listening to and receiving God's communicating love for us, always constant, never changing, yet always freshly being revealed to us in the circumstances of our human situation. This is how Jesus also experienced the triune love of God within Him and in His daily life.

THE FULLNESS OF GOD'S LOVE

GOD CANNOT INCREASE His love for us, for in Christ Jesus has He not given us the fullness of His love? Can the indwelling Trinity be imperfectly present in us? Does God wait for us to tell Him that we love Him and then He will come to us with a greater love? Does God's love for us become more ardent and perfect after we have performed for Him some good work? No! Prayer is not our attempt to change God so that He will love us more. It is our "tuning in" to God's all-pervasive presence as perfect love. It is to find Him in all things as the power that creates and sustains all creatures in being (Ac 17:29). The ultimate way we have of knowing how God loves us is to experience the love that Jesus has for us. This love is given to us as He dies on the cross freely for love of us. But also through His resurrection and the outpouring of His Holy Spirit, He pours that love of Himself and of His Father into our hearts through the Spirit they both give us (Rm 5:5).

The "good news" of the triune God living within us can come to us only through God's revelation, known in Holy Scripture and in the Church, which has received the knowledge and understanding to teach us prophetically with the mind of God. Through the mysteries of the incarnation, death and resurrection of the Word-made-flesh, and His giving to us a constant release of the Spirit of love, we can believe with certainty that, as we die to sin or self-love, we open ourselves up more and more to the eternal, Trinitarian community of love within and around us.

GOD WITHIN AND WITHOUT

THIS LOVING GOD TRULY INVADES US, no longer as an idea or a thought, but as the Source of all life. He drives out of our hearts every vestige of sin and darkness and transforms us into His loving light. As we get caught up inside of God's invading energies of love, we find ourselves gradually being consumed by the Trinity's mutual love for each other and for us. We become a prism through which God can radiate His love to all that we encounter. We become a magnifying glass — to use the example of the Gorlitz shoemaker and mystic, Jacob Boehme (+1624) — a magnifying glass that allows the rays of God's warm love to burst into flame and to engulf the world with godly love.

As we experience the transforming love of the triune God, we surrender more completely each day to be molded by the interior action of the Trinity. Our filial abandonment to the operations of the Trinity, as in the life of Jesus, is at once also a movement outward toward the world. From an anonymous world-community we move interiorly to meet the loving and personalized *We* community of Father, Son and Holy Spirit. The completion of that inner movement is an outward thrust back to the world community to be a servant through whom God can actualize a world community of *I, Thou and We*, the Body of Christ, the Church, ever conscious of being the Bride of Christ.

The degree of God's invasion of us, or rather of how much we surrender to allow His all-invading presence to transform us, is measured infallibly by the testimony of the fruit of the Holy Spirit produced in us as we relate to others (Gal 5:22). Love, peace, joy, gentleness, kindness, patience and forbearance are the result of our awareness that the Heavenly Father holds us in His two hands, Jesus Christ and His Spirit, and that He loves us infinitely. We show the presence and influence of the indwelling Trinity by the simple faith we have in the goodness of others who also are "invaded" by God. We trust others because we have let go of the control over our own lives in our surrender to God's interior guidance.

Compassionate mercy moves us, as it did Jesus, to bind up the wounds and to embrace the homeless of this world. The love of God in us gives us a share in God's love which is "always patient and kind; it is never jealous; love is never boastful or conceited; it is never rude or selfish; . . . it is always ready to excuse, to trust, to hope, and to endure whatever comes" (1 Cor 13:4-7).

In a word, to be invaded by God is to allow ourselves to be present to God who is everywhere. "In him we live and move and have our being" (Ac 17:28). It is to become so emptied of our nothingness and sinfulness that the Trinity may fill us with its richness, and through us re-create the world. It is not only to find the Trinity living within us, but it is to make the world around us present to the same immanently present and loving God, one in three.

The conclusion of Jesus' remark is that the Father loves Him so greatly and that He loves us with a similar emptying love. Then we should love one another in the same self-emptying manner even unto laying down our life if it is necessary in order to manifest such a divine love. Only in this manner of loving others, as Jesus and, therefore, the Father through the same Holy Spirit did, can we be called the friends of Jesus, His brothers and sisters, and really become true children of the Father in the Spirit:

> But I have called you friends, because I have made known to you all that I have heard from my Father. Not that you have chosen me: no, I have chosen you and the task I imposed upon you is to go forward steadfastly in bearing fruit; and your fruit is to be lasting. Thus the Father will grant you any petition you may present to him in my name. This is all I command you: love one another (Jn 15:15-17).

PRAYER

1. Jn 15:9-17	3. 1 Jn 3:1-6	5. Mt 25:31-46
2. Jn 13:31-38	4. 1 Jn 3:16-18	6. 1 Cor 13:1-13

21

"THE SPIRIT OF TRUTH . . . WILL WITNESS IN MY BEHALF" (Jn 15:26)

WE HAVE ALREADY SEEN that God is a community of love. The Father and the Son, the *I* and the *Thou*, live in each other

(Jn 10:38) through the bonding love of the Holy Spirit. Now John teaches us that we human beings can come to know the truth and the truth shall set us free. This truth is that the Father, the source and end of our being, through Jesus, God's Word incarnate, and His Spirit, whom the risen Lord sends into our hearts, loves us so much that He wants us to share in the very life and love of the Trinity. This same Holy Spirit will empower us to overcome the "sin" of the world which is unbelief in the truth that Jesus reveals to us about the infinite, self-emptying love of the Father for each of us. This the Spirit does by "witnessing" within our hearts through faith, hope and love, the truth about God's Trinitarian love for us. The same Spirit will give the disciples of Jesus the power to "witness" to this truth before the world, even in times of persecution for this truth, and thus be co-builders with the risen Jesus to fashion the world into the total Christ. Such a witness will reveal to the unbelievers that God's love is incarnate in the community of human beings, true disciples of Christ, as they love each other in the witness and empowerment of the Holy Spirit.

THE SPIRIT RESTS
UPON THE HUMAN JESUS

IN OUR CHOSEN TEXT from John's Gospel (15:18-16:33), Jesus intersperses between His promise of consolation to be given to His disciples in the face of the "world's" rejection and of actual persecution to those who follow Him, the promise to send His Advocate or Supporter, the Holy Spirit. Jesus, in His human consciousness, lived in the light of the Spirit's revelation and inner witness. For this reason the "world," those among the Jews of His day who did not believe the truth Jesus was witnessing to them of the Father's perfect love for them, persecuted Him even unto death. So also Jesus predicts future persecutions for His disciples if they live as witnesses to the truth.

The work of the Holy Spirit in the human life of Jesus was similar to His role within the Trinity. In the Trinity the role of the Holy Spirit is the loving, unifying bond that unites the Father to the Son and yet brings to each of the two Persons His unique personality. Speaking the Word in eternal silence through His outpouring love that is His Holy Spirit, the Heavenly Father hears His Word come back to Him in a perfect, eternal, "yes" of total, surrendering Love, that is again the Holy Spirit. The Spirit "proceeds" from the union of the two, uniquely different Persons, Father and Son. His being as a Person, the hidden, "kenotic" element within the Trinity, consists in being the act of union and distinction between the Father and Son and in this "action" the Spirit finds His personhood.

In the humility of Jesus, the Father poured His Spirit of love into His being. The baptism of Jesus in the Jordan gives us a model of the progress of Jesus' human development over His whole life, climaxing in the cross and resurrection. Jesus receives a vision as He comes out of the water, seeing the Spirit as a gentle dove and hearing His Father declare from on high: "You are my Son, the Beloved, my favor rests on you" (Mk 1:11). The heavens opened and Jesus is made aware in His human consciousness that He is hearing His Heavenly Father and seeing the Holy Spirit come upon Him as the Father's Gift.

He is swept up into an ecstatic oneness with the Father. Like the water that flows down over his human body, so the love of the Father for Him as his beloved Son cascades over Him and covers Him with His glory. Heaven and earth had been closed by man's first sin in the garden. Now God's communicating presence has passed through the barrier of sin, and Jesus, God's holiness, takes His place in solidarity with the human family.

The Spirit leads Jesus into the *truth*, namely, the joyful and peaceful assurance that the Father loves Him in His human nature with the very same self-emptying love of the Father for His only begotten Son within the Trinity, as revealed by the Holy Spirit.

"THE SPIRIT WILL WITNESS IN MY BEHALF"

Now Jesus reveals to His disciples and to us who follow in their revelation through faith that:

> When the Advocate whom I am going to send you with a mission from the Father — the Spirit of truth, who proceeds from the Father — has come, he will witness in my behalf. And you, too, will witness, because you have been with me from the beginning (Jn 15:26-27).

The role of the Holy Spirit to *witness* and the power to make the disciples of Jesus also *witnesses* to the world play an important part in the Johannine theology of the Spirit. The first witnessing on the part of the Holy Spirit is to give members of the community of love, the Body of Christ, the infusion of faith, hope and love that will "convict" them that Jesus is Lord (1 Cor 12:4) and that the risen Jesus lives in them (1 Jn 3:21).

The second witnessing is the empowering by the Spirit of the followers of Jesus to become themselves witnesses before the world of what they have experienced interiorly through the personalized witnessing of the Spirit. The two types of witnessing through the Holy Spirit, interior and exterior before the world, go together since there is the same Spirit and the same truth witnessed to. Jesus shows His disciples the great advantage in His departure from them in His human form through His death, for only then can He send the Supporter.

"And when he comes, he will show the world the meaning of guilt, of innocence, and of condemnation; guilt — they do not believe in me; innocence — I am going home to the Father and you will see me no longer; condemnation — the prince of this world stands condemned" (Jn 16:8-11).

Thus the Holy Spirit makes a new understanding of the basis of all reality accessible to those who believe. The importance of the Holy Spirit as Gift in building the Christian community is highlighted in this passage. The community from now on must deal only with the word of Jesus in the preaching of the Church. But this must not sadden the disciples nor be a disadvantage for future believers. The basic movement for the twelve disciples and for future believers is the same. The decisive step in any encounter with Jesus is a movement from unbelief to faith. The Spirit's action is wholly related to the activity of Jesus. We could say that Jesus lives and returns as revelation of the Father's immense love for His children in the person of the Holy Spirit. The physical, material existence of Jesus on this earth is now replaced by His presence as risen Lord through the Spirit.

The main work of the Spirit of the risen Jesus is described in the words spoken by Jesus in this farewell discourse as a "witnessing" of the Spirit in the hearts of the disciples: "When the Advocate whom I am going to send you with a mission from the Father — the Spirit of truth, who proceeds from the Father — has come, he will witness in my behalf. And you, too, will witness, because you have been with me from the beginning" (Jn 15:27).

The witnessing of the Spirit — both in the hearts of the followers of Jesus and in their exteriorly witnessing the Spirit's revealed truth — takes place on three levels: "He will show the

world the meaning of guilt, of innocence, and of condemnation. . ." (Jn 16:8-9). The Spirit will point out the guilt of the
"world," meaning the forces of unbelief in what Jesus came to
reveal about the Triune God's love for mankind. Thus the Spirit
will strengthen the faith of the disciples down through the
centuries on the interior level. By "convicting" the world of
unbelief in Jesus as the fullness of the Father's revelation of love
for this world, the Spirit will also convince the followers of Jesus
that deliberate unbelief in Him is the root of all sin. He also
convinces them that Jesus has entered into glory by going back
to the Father, and is thus more present to them as through the
Spirit He brings the fullness of the revelation of the Father to His
disciples. This Spirit will reveal to the hearts of the disciples all
that Jesus has ever said or done, who He really is: the true Son
of God, the perfect image, especially in His death on the cross,
of the Father's perfect love for each of us.

Not only does the Spirit witness to the world's guilt for
rejecting Jesus, but the Spirit witnesses to justice or innocence
in the fact that Jesus is going to the Father. The harmony God
had foreseen when He created all things out of love to exist in a
unity of love is being reestablished by Jesus' being glorified and
lifted up to the Father's right hand to become the powerful
intercessor of the entire human and created world. Victory has
already been won by Jesus. The world will see Jesus as absent;
the believers of Jesus will see Him as the conquering Son of
God to whom all power in heaven and on earth has been given.

And for this reason, the Spirit witnesses to the condemnation of the prince of this world (Jn 16:11). The disciples of Jesus
were saddened at the thought of His departure. But Jesus holds
out to them the hope of His paschal victory. Through their
witnessing, this victory over the forces of evil is to be made
available to all in the world unto final victory. The world has no
victory over Jesus or His followers. They will be emboldened
preachers of His word, as we see in Acts. "And the Lord

accompanied them with his power enabling them to heal and work miracles through the name of Jesus" (Ac 4:29-31).

BUILDER OF A WORLD COMMUNITY

NOT ONLY DOES THE HOLY SPIRIT BUILD up the community of believers in the face of worldly difficulties and persecutions, but through the Spirit the disciples down through the ages have been given an ever-deeper understanding of the message and the medium of God's revelation, i.e. Jesus Christ. He does not propose any new teachings, but the Spirit of truth does give Christian followers of Jesus a more profound understanding of the mystery of Jesus, of His life, actions and words and their meaning for daily living.

Thus this Spirit is our Consoler and Comforter, our strength and power as we go out into the world of unbelief — even that world of darkness and distrust of God's revelation in Jesus Christ — to drive out the spirit of the world by our child-like confidence in the Lord given to us by His Holy Spirit. ". . . at present you are in sorrow; but I shall see you again, and then your hearts will rejoice and no one will take your joy away from you" (Jn 16:22). Joy is the true index of the interior witness of the Spirit within our hearts of the Good News of Jesus. It is also the touchstone of the exterior witness of the Spirit that, amidst persecutions from "unbelievers," we may rejoice and be glad for the kingdom of Heaven is already a reality.

PRAYER

1. Jn 15:18-16:33
2. Jn 14:16-31
3. Jn 20:21-23
4. 1 Jn 4:12-21
5. Rm 8:14-27
6. Gal 4:4-7

22

"THE FATHER
LOVES YOU DEARLY" (Jn 16:27)

JESUS HAS REVEALED to His disciples and to us that, as the Father loves Him, so He loves us (Jn 15:9). Now He reveals the basis for all Christian happiness and joy. "Of his own accord the Father loves you dearly, because you are settled in your love for me and in your conviction that I come from the Father. I come from the Father and have come into the world. And now I am leaving the world and going home to the Father" (Jn 16:27-29).

God is love (1 Jn 4:8). Now through the gift of the Holy Spirit, sent to Jesus' disciples down through the ages, we Christians can believe with absolute certainty that the almighty, omnipotent God is a community of love. God is a family made up of self-sacrificing, self-emptying acts of love between the Father and the Son through the Spirit.

But, much more! This community of three distinct but inseparable Persons is always present, immanently loving us with the same love of the originating, Trinitarian community. This community we carry within each of us, twenty-four hours a day! God, Trinity, loves us!

RESULTS OF FAITH

OUR FAITH, however, in Jesus' revelation that He and the Father truly love us is revealed in the "new time," the "Day of Yahweh," which for us Christians is now the Resurrection and

Pentecost. Jesus risen and the Heavenly Father are now, after Easter, present to us in the community, the Church, the Body of Christ. This greatest of all realities is revealed to us, not once in an intellectual assent, but in our ongoing call to respond in the circumstances of our worldly existence in human, historical time and space by a similar self-emptying love.

JOY, NO ONE CAN TAKE AWAY

JESUS POINTS OUT what effects accompany the degree of our faith-response to the Father's and the Son's love for us as revealed in each moment by the Holy Spirit. In His resurrectional presence His disciples would see Him through the release of His Spirit in their hearts. ". . . But I shall see you again, and then your hearts will rejoice, and no one will take your joy away from you" (Jn 16:22).

In spite of their being "in the world" and always subjected to persecutions for their belief in Him, their joy will be constant. The pivotal truth and basis for their joy is that the Father loves them dearly (16:27). The Spirit enkindles in their hearts the fire of joy and peace stemming from the primary gift of God's triune love for each of them.

NEW KNOWLEDGE

ANOTHER EFFECT of this awareness of God's triune love for them is that Jesus' disciples will not need to ask Him any more questions (Jn 16:23). For all Christians, living in a world cloaked with darkness and ignorance and the sin of unbelief in Jesus as the Son of the Father, there must be questions asked if faith is to be an ongoing response to God's love for us. We need to follow Augustine's lead: "I became a question to myself."

The question we must ask is: "Shall I respond to my Heavenly Father's perfect love for me in this moment?" The apostles in our text had been approaching the departure of Jesus intellectually. They were asking one question after another with no peace and joy, since they were expecting intellectual answers. Jesus was leading them to seek the answers which faith alone could give. When they accept this new knowledge, they will have no need to ask any further questions.

Faith in the Father's love for them will require no other questions since it will bring them the "final" explanation. "Of his own accord the Father loves you dearly, because you are settled in your love for me and in your conviction that I come from the Father" (Jn 16:27).

EFFECTIVE PRAYER

WITH SUCH FAITH in the Father's love we, too, are taught by Him to put aside all questions about the *how, when, where* and *why*. "That will be the time when you ask me no more questions. It is the real truth when I tell you that, if you make any request to the Father, he will grant it to you in my name. Up to the present you made no requests in my name. Make them, and they will be granted. Thus nothing will be wanting to your joy" (Jn 16:23-24).

Jesus had explained to the disciples and to the crowds who listened to Him how to enter into the Kingdom of Heaven. "You, therefore, must not be anxious about your food and drink, or live in constant suspense. Why, the heathens, all the world over, make all these things an object of eager search; but you have a Father who knows that you need these things. Instead, make his kingdom your concern; then you will have those other things thrown in for good measure" (Lk 12:29-31).

Now our criterion of effective prayer is not whether God answers all our questions (which He will not do!) and grants all our requests which we may petition the Father in Jesus' name, but whether our will is one with God's when we pray. Generally our petitions flow from our "carnal mind" and not out of a Spirit-filled heart. To ask the Father in Jesus' name is to ask in union with the risen Lord, as persons who are one in Christ. The Father sees us living in a unity of love with Jesus. We are totally surrendered to let Jesus be our Head, we His members. We obey His word. We say our *fiat*, that His word be done in us.

Therefore, the test of our effective prayer can no longer be what *we* want but what He wills. We are to answer the question, "Do I really, with 'passionate indifference,' accept Jesus as the infallible Revealer and Mediator before the Father?"

If we in prayer and in each moment respond to the Father's love, then truly all things will be granted to us because we trust in Him since we *know* now by a new knowledge of faith, hope and love that we are one with Jesus risen and He is one with the Father. Jesus through His death and resurrection has conquered "sin and death" and opened us up to become sharers with Him of a *new creation*. "If, then, any man is in Christ, he is a new creation; the old state of things has gone; wonderful to tell, it has been made over, absolutely new. All this comes from the action of God, who has reconciled us to himself through Christ, and has entrusted us with this ministry of reconciliation" (2 Cor 5:17-18).

A CHILD OF GOD

UNITED IN LOVE with the risen Jesus, we have His Spirit to witness within our "hearts," at the deepest level of our consciousness, that we really are children of God (Rm 8:15; Gal 4:6; 1 Jn 3:1). The Spirit reveals that we live in Jesus Christ, the

only begotten Son of the Father. Jesus releases His Spirit
through His resurrectional power and glory so that we are now
incorporated into a loving, unified community with Jesus as our
head.

His Spirit empowers us to call the Father of Jesus *Abba*,
since we form one body with Jesus before the Father. St. Paul
understood this "organic" oneness of the individual Christian
living "in Christ" when he wrote:

> He came and announced the Good News of peace to you who were
> afar off, and of peace to those who were near, because by one and the
> same Spirit through him both of us have found entrance to the Father. It
> follows that you are no longer foreigners and guests; no, you are fellow
> citizens with the saints, and members of God's household. You are an
> edifice built on the foundation of the apostles and prophets with Christ
> Jesus himself as the chief cornerstone. In him the whole structure is
> being closely fitted together by the Spirit to become God's temple
> consecrated in the Lord. In him you, too, are being fitted by the Spirit
> into the edifice to become God's dwelling place (Ep 2:17-22).

As Jesus belongs to the family of God by virtue of His
eternal, divine sonship with the Father, so by His Spirit we
Christians, one with Jesus, also through the Spirit's grace, now
belong to God's triune family. United with Christ, we share
God's very own life within us. Jesus is the brother of us all and
He makes it possible through His Spirit to live as His brothers
and sisters since we have the same Heavenly Father!

JOYFUL TRUST IN THE FATHER

BECAUSE THE SPIRIT WITNESSES within us in each moment that we
have a loving Father, we can experience His perfect love for us
in each circumstance of our lives. Words like "pleasant" or
"unpleasant," "success" or "failure" have little meaning now

for the Christian who has been converted. God is our Father. He will care for us. We are to become like a little child (Mt 18:3-4).

We have mentioned earlier the beautiful concept of *parrhesia* which the Greek Fathers developed as of one piece with Jesus' revelation to us of the Father's great love for each of us. Once the risen Lord releases His Spirit into our hearts and convinces us that we truly are children of God, we have absolute certainty in all circumstances of life that our Father truly loves us, actively and tenderly.

The apostles after Pentecost are described in Acts as possessing *parrhesia,* a childlike frankness and directness coupled with certain knowledge and no more parables or inferences, to preach the message of Jesus fearlessly and boldly. "And now, Lord, consider their threats, and grant to your servants courage to speak your message with complete and firm assurance while you exercise your power to effect cures, signs, and wonders to be wrought by the name of your holy servant Jesus" (Ac 4:29-30).

No threat to their lives, no trials, persecutions, imprisonment, nothing could make them fear since they possessed an inner joy and childlike trust in their all-loving and all-powerful Father.

Such childlike trust (*parrhesia*) before their Heavenly Father, gave them an inner dignity as they petitioned the Father. They were able to intercede directly before the Father. The reason for their ability to intercede on behalf of others to heal and perform miracles is always the same that Jesus revealed to them: the Father loves them because they have loved Jesus and were convinced that He came as the true Son of the Father (Jn 16:27).

Such childlike, almost naive trust in the Father's constant love makes them humbly one with Jesus before the Father. The Father, however, does not merely love us as He loves Jesus. He

sees us in our intimate union with Jesus, and He sees us in all
our very personal uniqueness. Christ is the Head and we the
members. We live no longer for ourselves, but Christ lives in us
(Gal 2:20) and we joyfully surrender ourselves to the infinite,
perfect love of the Father. Jesus has given us the truth! And to
live in this truth of the Father's love for us is *parrhesia*, the
childlike, humble boldness, a playful joyfulness that knows no
sadness because our Father dearly loves us!

PRAYER

1. Jn 16:19-33   3. Jn 5:36-47   5. 1 Jn 3:1-10
2. Jn 17:6-8   4. Gal 4:1-7   6. Ep 2:17-22

23

"AND THIS IS THE SUM
OF ETERNAL LIFE — THEIR KNOWING YOU, THE ONLY
TRUE GOD, AND YOUR AMBASSADOR JESUS CHRIST"
(Jn 17:3)

If JESUS throughout His earthly existence lived in a loving
surrender to His Heavenly Father, how much more do we
discover this in Jesus' final farewell prayer to His Father and in
the actual completion of that prayer in His death-glorification
on the cross! The goal of His life is to make His Father our

Father, to be God's revelation and our savior, making this revelation known and experienced by all mankind.

Now He gathers with His disciples before His death and His heart is turned intensely toward His Father. We have seen already that John gives us two farewell discourses by way of teaching His followers. The first farewell discourse is found in John 13:31 to 14:31. The second is in John 15:1 to 16:33. Now, in our text of His final farewell, Jesus no longer deals with instructional information.

He has answered all questions. So the evangelist provides the reader with a "way" into the very heart of Christ by presenting Jesus' most prolonged prayer found in the Gospels. This is His farewell prayer or, as it has been often called, the high-priestly prayer of Jesus.

TURNED TOWARD THE FATHER

JESUS IS REPORTED PRAYING OFTEN in the Gospels. But in this prayer Jesus allows us, as it were, to eavesdrop on this very intimate colloquy with the Father. He faces the Father with a filial heart full of adoration. Overcome by the Father's majesty and power, but also by His tender love for His Son, Jesus is full of gratitude and self-surrender to the Father in total commitment to do His holy will. He is grateful for all that the Father has done in His life and will do in the final hours of His earthly existence. The entire Chapter 17, therefore, constitutes an extended prayer of three parts: a prayer for His glorification and that of His Father through His revelation to His disciples of the truth of God's love within the Trinity and for the world; then a prayer for His disciples who would be left behind in the world that they may be one in sharing the oneness which He has had from all eternity with the Father; and finally, a prayer for the Christian community down through the centuries that would accept His revelation given to the world through His chosen disciples.

Jesus raises His eyes toward heaven. He lifts us up to the "place" where the Father is present to His children. In that "place" Jesus had lived out His entire human existence. The Father, *Abba*, of Jesus, was His center or the core to which Jesus easily turned in every thought, word and deed. All was aligned in Jesus' consciousness in oneness of loving adoration with the Father. "I have glorified you on earth by completing the work you gave me to do" (Jn 17:4).

Now Jesus prays that in the "hour" that is approaching, namely, His death and resurrection, He Himself would be glorified. "Glorify your Son that your Son may glorify you" (Jn 17:1). The glorification of Jesus by the Father and of the Father by Him has to be seen in John's Gospel as the summary of John's teaching about God as a Trinitarian community of love as revealed in the human "works" of Jesus.

GLORIFICATION

WHAT DOES THE GLORIFICATION of the Father and the Son mean? We have all too long conceived Jesus' role in His humanity as a paying back to the Father the enormous debt we have contracted by our sins. We think that Jesus, in doing God's will by dying on the cross in our behalf, gives the Father glory, something extrinsic to the Trinity. We, therefore, conceive our earthly task coming from our oneness with Christ as also to render God extrinsic glory.

The Johannine concept of the glorification of God the Father, the Son and *ourselves*, for which Jesus prays in this last, most extended prayer in John 17, offers us a much different view. For John, the hour in which Jesus is to be glorified by the Father is the hour of His death and resurrection by which the

Father gives Jesus His due as the Son of God. This is not an external honor bestowed upon Jesus for obeying the Father by dying on the cross for us. It means that the Father accepts the incarnate Word, the God-Man, as sharing the divine *shekinah* or light and splendor that constitutes the inner life of the Trinitarian community of love.

St. Paul expresses this beautiful concept, so difficult to present in simple human words, when he writes:

> This is why God has exalted him and given him the name above all names, so that at the name of Jesus everyone in heaven, on earth, and beneath the earth should bend the knee and should publicly acknowledge to the glory of God the Father that Jesus Christ is Lord (Ph 2:9-11).

Glorification of Jesus by the Father and that of the Father by Jesus takes place at the moment of God's greatest revelation of who God is and what He is in relationship to us, His children. This happens in that momentless moment on the cross, that new time, *kairos*, that catches for all eternity the permanent presence of God in Jesus who now means for us what His name in Hebrew indicates: God who saves.

LOVE BETWEEN
THE FATHER AND THE SON

WHEN JOHN USES the word *glory*, he is calling us to enter radically into the light of God's Spirit who reveals to us beyond any human concepts that God's glory equals the revelation or unveiling of the love between the Father and the Son.

Jesus, stretched out on the cross, His blood poured out unto the last drop, is at the same moment bathed in the glory of God's perfect love. The implosive self-emptying love of the

Father toward the Son and the Son toward the Father in the personalized, *kenotic* love of the hidden, humble Spirit, is manifested to the world as exploding love unto death.

Death and resurrection go together. God's glory is the fullest manifestation in human terms of the creative, suffering love revealed by the God-Man. Jesus is glorifed by the Father, but as the fullest embodiment of what God is truly like. "As the Father has loved me, so I love you" (Jn 15:9).

AUTHORITY GIVEN TO JESUS

EARLIER IN HIS GOSPEL John had written: "Just as the Father is the source of life, so, too, has he given the Son the power to be a source of life; and he has authorized him to pass judgment, because he is a son of man" (Jn 5:26-27). Now Jesus tells us in His prayer to the Father: "You have given him authority over all mankind, that he might give eternal life to all you have entrusted to him" (7:2).

The authority that Jesus has from the Father is not to pass judgment on what others have done of good or evil, but, rather, to bring others to eternal life. His authority comes from His being the perfect image of the Father revealing the healing love of the Trinity for all God's children.

Individuals will judge themselves by accepting or rejecting Jesus Christ as the light, reflecting God's glory to us. "And just as Moses lifted up the serpent in the desert, so the Son of Man must needs be lifted up, that everyone who believes in him may have eternal life" (Jn 3:14-15).

God the Father and Jesus, His Son, are glorified when the world can look up and see God's love fully manifested in the suffering servant of Yahweh on the cross.

ETERNAL LIFE

JOHN USES THIS PHRASE, *eternal life*, as another way of expressing salvation. This is revealed objectively by Jesus through His death-resurrection and the outpouring of the Spirit who witnesses, to us who choose to be baptized by Jesus in His Spirit, that Jesus is truly the revealed Word of God. It is subjectively accepted and acted upon by those whom the Father has entrusted to Jesus (Jn 17:2). Succinctly John then describes in what this eternal life consists:

> And this is the sum of eternal life — their knowing you, the only true God, and your ambassador Jesus Christ (Jn 17:3).

This eternal life John describes by using Greek gnostic terms of inner knowledge or *gnosis*. John means that this life of knowing by participation in the triune life of the Father, Son and Holy Spirit is not merely to be bestowed upon us, the followers of Jesus, at the end of the world. It is already an eternal gift of God's life to us in this present, historical moment. It is made possible through the revealing gift of Jesus Christ who is God the Father's gift of Himself to us.

This is highlighted in John's First Epistle:

> I refer to the Word who is and who imparts life. Indeed, this life has manifested himself. We ourselves have seen and testify and proclaim that Eternal Life which was with the Father and has manifested himself. To you we proclaim what we have seen and heard, that you may share our treasure with us. That treasure is union with the Father and his Son, Jesus Christ. I write this to you that we may have joy in the fullest measure (1 Jn 1:1-4).

KNOWING IS LOVING

THE EARLY GREEK FATHERS UNDERSTOOD John's knowledge or *gnosis* of the Father and the Son through the Spirit as an ongoing, experiential knowledge beyond our cognitive understanding. In such a knowledge given by the Spirit, *gnosis* is equivalent to *agape*, God's perfect, outpoured love for us. This process of experiencing God's perfect love unto death for us brings a transformation the early Fathers called divinization or *theosis*, our becoming *gods* by grace as we are transformed into true children of God (1 Jn 3:1; Rm 8:15-19; Gal 4:6). We become sharers of God's perfect life that knows no boundaries and lies beyond the ravages of death.

Revelation of eternal life by Jesus in John's theology is intimately connected with the actual communication and participation in the indwelling life of the Trinity. This is the aim and purpose of why the Eternal Word, in whom "was life and the life was the light of men" (Jn 1:4), pitched His tent among us. "But to as many as welcomed him he gave the power to become children of God — those who believe in his name; who were born not of blood, or of carnal desire, or of man's will; no, they were born of God" (1:12-13).

This is the "work" the Father gave Jesus to do on earth (Jn 17:4). Now Jesus prays that the Father glorify Him in His bosom "with the glory I possessed in your bosom before the world existed" (17:5). John in this final prayer comes full circle to what he traced out in summary fashion in his Prologue.

The Good News is that God is not only one, "the only true God" (Jn 17:3), but through His ambassador, Jesus Christ, God is *di-polar*. He is transcendent and absolute subsistence in Himself. Yet He is supremely *relative*. He contains the possibilities of giving "otherness" to beings in His transcendence; yet He also immanently possesses the ability to want and to actually receive a return of love from His human creatures. God is eternal, but also active and receptive in creation and redemption. He is impassible, but also "passible." He is the "inside," immanent ground of all beings, not out of an essential "need" or imperfect dependence upon creatures to complete Himself, but because He, as a Trinitarian community of love, has freely chosen to "other" the same self-emptying love found within the Trinity outside into His created world.

God freely chooses to "limit" Himself to bring others into being in time and space. He freely limits Himself to wait upon our free response to receive a share in His "eternal life." We are worthwhile in God's eyes. He waits for our loving response. He is affected by our decisions. We may be sinful, "black," but still we are "lovely" as the Song of Songs describes. We share in the *already* of God's eternal life and the *not yet* of our transformation by cooperating with God's self-gift (Sg 1:5).

The secret of our transformation and our impacting the world by our own creativity in oneness with the infinite creativity of God is that we experience God's personal, loving activity in the events of our daily lives. This is why Jesus Christ alone is the *Way* that leads us to God as *kenotic* love. We human beings through Jesus Christ can now believe that, as He suffers for us, especially by dying on the cross for us, so we now have an image of how great is God's desire to pour Himself out in associating with our sufferings. Jesus becomes our "fellow-sufferer" and chooses humbly to be like God. It is the most perfect plan of imaging the eternal love of the Father for us. We have no other way of knowing the interiority of the incomprehensible God except through the revelation of the Son. In Him as involved, suffering love, freely given for us, we have the perfect expression in human language of the very being of God.

Such knowledge must come to us as a gift through the Supporter, the Holy Spirit, who reveals that God's love must be dialogical. The Father is always speaking His Word to us. Jesus is always loving us unto death. He is now present in our lives with that same dynamic, eternal love which He had when He died to serve us and which He had from all eternity in the bosom of the Father. In the context of our daily lives we dialogue with God's revealing Word as emptying love. Such an experience in daily living leads us into the awesome presence of the Heavenly Father as perfect holiness, beauty and love. We live by the exhortation of St. Paul: ". . . and the reason he died for all was so that living men should live no longer for themselves, but for him who died and was raised to life for them" (2 Cor 5:15). This truly is already eternal life, the glorification of the Father and the Son and ourselves as we all participate more and more in the Trinity's very own life and love. All this is the "work" the Father gave to His Son, Jesus Christ, our Revealer and Savior. "It is the same God that said: 'Let there be light shining out of darkness,' who has shone in our minds to radiate the light of the knowledge of God's glory, the glory on the face of Christ" (2 Cor 4:6).

PRAYER

1. Jn 17:1-5   3. Jn 5:19-47   5. 1 Jn 1:1-4
2. Jn 1:1-18   4. Jn 8:21-30   6. Ezk 36:16-38

24

"ALL ARE TO BE ONE;
JUST AS YOU, FATHER, ARE IN ME AND I AM IN YOU,
SO THEY, TOO, ARE TO BE ONE IN US. THE WORLD
MUST COME TO BELIEVE THAT I AM YOUR
AMBASSADOR" (Jn 17:21)

WHAT MAKES CHRISTIANITY a unique religion over all others is its
accent on love that, as Teilhard de Chardin writes, differentiates as it unites. For Christians love is passionate *desire*,
the desire to empty oneself of all independent security and
isolation in order to "pass-over" in availability and self-gift on
behalf of others. God is love (1 Jn 4:8) and love unfolds within a
community of an *I-Thou-We*, encircled within each other, and
discovering always new and more exciting levels of awareness
of each of the Trinitarian family's uniqueness in the very oneness of unity.

We have shown that John's constant message is that Jesus
is the Light shining in the darkness of our sinful world and
bringing us a share in the Trinity's very own communitarian
love and life. Now in our present text we see another of John's
constant themes. To the degree that we have come to know by
the infused knowledge given us by the Holy Spirit through the
gifts of faith, hope and love the perfect, constant love of God for
us through Jesus Christ in His Spirit, to that degree can we
become truly regenerated "from above" by the Holy Spirit.
Through the divinization process we are to become transformed into God's very own children. And in our new oneness

in the risen Lord, we are to build a similar new creation, the New Jerusalem, by our readiness to love all others as Jesus loves us.

Jesus ends His farewell prayer to the Father as He ardently prays for His intimate disciples that they may be guarded from the spirit of the "world" and live in loving oneness just as He and the Father live in oneness. He includes in His prayer all other believers who will receive His revelation, that they all may be one as He and the Father are "in" each other.

"THEY ARE MY CROWNING GLORY"

THUS WE WITNESS the burning love Jesus has, not only for each individual apostle, but for all His followers down through the centuries. He prays for those in His present oneness with them before He enters into His "hour." He prays for those in the future who through His twelve chosen disciples will come to believe His revelation.

Jesus declares to His Father why He is praying for His disciples. First, they belong to the Father. "Yours they were and to me you have entrusted them. . ." (Jn 17:6). What belongs to the Father also belongs to the Son. The disciples belong truly to Jesus in a most endearing way.

Another reason why Jesus prays for His disciples is that He Himself will be glorified in them since "they cherish your message. Now they know that whatever you have given me really comes from you; for the message you have delivered to me I have delivered to them; and they have accepted it. They really understand that I come from you, and they believe that I am your ambassador" (Jn 17:8). A final reason for His prayer is that He is tenderly concerned with His disciples since He is about to leave them. He wishes that the Father protect them from "unbelief," which is the Johannine concept of the sin of the "world." "I am not long for this world; but they remain in the world; while I am about to return to you" (17:11).

"HOLY FATHER"

JESUS ADDRESSES His Father as "holy." In this final prayer, Jesus calls His Father by the simple title of "Father" (Jn 17:5, 21, 24) and as "just Father" (17:25). Here He speaks to His "holy Father" (17:11), which brings us into many deep insights concerning Jesus' prayer for the unity of His followers.

To address God as *holy* in Scripture, especially in the Old Testament, is more than describing one of His special divine qualities. It is the Old Testament way of depicting the very essence of God. To describe God's holiness is to touch the "insideness" of God. God's power can be seen in His creative works of nature. But God's holiness is God in His perfection as good and beautiful and loving. It is, above all, God in the totality of His being, moving outwardly toward the other, toward human and angelic persons to offer Himself as gift.

In Holy Scripture, whenever God is described as holy, He is always close to human beings or angels, involved in communicating His loving nature so that His very life may be shared in a union of love.

> For it is I, Yahweh, who am your God. You have been sanctified and have become holy because I am holy. . . . Yes, it is I, Yahweh, who have brought you out of Egypt to be your God: you, therefore, must be holy because I am holy (Lv 11:44-45).

Isaiah was swept up in vision before the throne of God and saw how the Seraphs covered their faces and feet and cried out constantly: "Holy, holy, holy is Yahweh Sabaoth. His glory fills the whole earth" (Is 6:3). Moses fell back before the holiness of

Yahweh in the burning bush. For that was *holy* ground (Ex 3:4-6), because God who is holy made Himself present in that place. No human hand could touch the Ark of the Covenant because God's holy presence was in that place. His holiness was localized in the Inner Sanctum, in the Holy of Holies, for it was there Yahweh promised to enter into His special, loving communication with His people.

God creates, but He is more perfectly present to us human beings when His holiness touches us to sanctify us. God's holy presence is God, entering upon a self-giving that allows us to become sharers, through love, in His very own nature. This has always been the end of our lives. ". . . be holy in all you do, since it is the Holy One who has called you, and scripture says: Be holy, for I am holy" (1 P 1:15-16).

God calls us to receive His holiness and to become holy as He is, to open ourselves to his outpouring love and gift of Himself for us, and then to become outpoured gift in love of Him and neighbor. We are called to be saints, or holy people, sanctified by God's holiness (Rm 1:7; 1 Cor 1:2). "We have been called by God to be holy, not to be immoral" (1 Th 4:7). God chose us from the beginning to be holy by the sanctifying power of the Holy Spirit (2 Th 2:13), "chose us in Christ to be *holy* and spotless, and to live through love in his presence, determining that we should become his adopted sons through Jesus Christ. . ." (Ep 1:4-5).

JESUS IS HOLY AS HIS FATHER

JESUS COMES IN HUMAN FORM to act out God's holiness. Now we know the answer to the question: What is God's holiness like? It is like the holiness of Jesus. The holiness of Jesus consists first in His having been sanctified by the Holy Spirit. He was the gift of the Father through the Spirit. That Spirit quickened in Jesus' consciousness an ever-increased awareness that He and the Father were one in the same Spirit of love. It is the Father who has sent Him into the world and consecrated Him, made Him holy in order to bring God's holiness to the world (Jn 10:36). "As you have made me your ambassador to the world, so I am making them my ambassadors to the world; and for their sake I consecrate myself, that they, in turn, may in reality be consecrated" (Jn 17:18-19).

Jesus shows us His holiness and the imaged holiness of His Father in His self-giving to each individual who has a need. He lives to remove from human lives any pain or suffering and to replace it with exuberant, rich, happy health and fulfillment. His service is love enacted, even unto His death.

The holiness of Jesus reaches its peak when He is about to die freely as a victim. He offered freely Himself, the High Priest, on the cross, that we might see the depths of His holiness. In this final prayer of His we see the heart of Jesus turned prayerfully to the Father. He prays for the holiness of His disciples and those who would follow them down through the centuries.

HOLINESS IN UNITY

THEIR HOLINESS would be witnessed to in the world precisely by their living in a community of love which would reflect the Trinitarian holiness of divine self-emptying love for them. Such "holy" self-giving John shows to be the basis of the witness of Jesus' followers. The test of the authenticity of such a community of love would be the unity shown within that community in which Jesus and His Spirit would be operating along with the members' cooperation. St. Paul captures a similar relationship between loving service and unity as a witness of the triune love experienced by the Christian community.

Have patience and bear lovingly with one another. Strive anxiously to preserve harmony of mind by means of the bond which effects peace. There is one body and one Spirit, even as you, from the moment you were called, had the one hope your calling imparted. There is one Lord, one faith, one Baptism, one God and Father of all, who rules all things and pervades all things and sustains all things (Ep 4:2-6).

The Johannine Jesus, in His prayer for oneness among His disciples of all ages, sees such unity never as static or a unity that can be possessed once and forever but rather as something that has to be achieved ever anew. Nor can it ever be imposed by any extrinsic hierarchical authority. It must go beyond a mere material oneness in faith and morals to unity in worship and sacraments as well as unanimity in obedience to ecclesiastical authority.

The unity Jesus prays for in His last farewell prayer comes from within the basic community of all reality and all love, the Trinity. We human beings cannot attain this unity by our own exclusive efforts or by mere methods of organization. It comes only through the members of the Body of Christ first abiding in a loving union with Jesus.

Jesus prays and intercedes for His disciples within the very Christian community that this spiritual unity may be ever more realized in an ongoing process. He knows that His Father's love for Him and the Father's love for His disciples is the selfsame love. Unity among the members comes primarily as a gift from the Trinity.

> The glory you have bestowed on me
> I have bestowed on them,
> that they may be one as we are one,
> I in them and you in me.
> Thus their oneness will be perfected.
> The world must come to acknowledge
> that I am your ambassador,
> and that you love them as you love me (Jn 17:22-23)

Thus we see that John never views as two distinct and separable relationships Christians relating individually to God vertically and then horizontally toward each other. The unity of believers with the Trinity and their communion with one another have one and the same originating source, the one life and love shared between the Father and the Son in their mutual Holy Spirit.

A VISIBLE UNITY

YET SUCH A UNITY can never be merely interior or invisible in an exclusively spiritual way. Over and over the Johannine Jesus mentions in this prayer the concrete fraternal love (Jn 17:23, 26) and its similarity (17:21) to His great command: "A new commandment I give you: love one another; as I love you, so I want you, too, to love one another. By this token all the world must know that you are my disciples — by cherishing love for one another" (Jn 13:34-35).

Today ecumenical and church leaders must keep this basic truth ever in mind as they dialogue in an attempt to attain unity among all members of the true Body of Christ. It is only God's gift of love through the Holy Spirit that can effect any degree of unity among Christ's followers. We human beings can never by good will bring this about since it is the free gift of the radical communion of love, the Trinity, to us.

Yet we Christians must cooperate by witnessing to this intense and perfect love of the Trinity that flows from within us outward toward the world. Such unity in God we already possess objectively.

What is impossible for us to attain merely through our feeble human efforts is possible with our humble cooperation with the very triune energies of divine love within us. There will always be a dynamic tension between unity and plurality, between the oneness of all in Christ and the uniqueness of each individual member.

For this reason Jesus ends His beautiful prayer by petitioning the Father that all who follow Him will enter into the fullness of the glory which He Himself has known in His oneness with the Father from all eternity. We reach out amidst our brokenness and infidelity to the loving Trinity and to all our brothers and sisters throughout God's creation. And we struggle for that perfect unity which awaits us more fully in the life to come. The promise is already being answered as we carry out the two great commands which bring about this perfect unity of the one and the many, as in the Trinity: love God with our whole heart (Dt 6:6) and love our neighbor as ourselves (Lv 19:18) through the love of the Trinity which transforms us into greater and greater oneness with Jesus Christ.

This is the conclusion of Jesus' prayer to the Father, the goal and future promise of what is already ours, but not quite yet, in all its fullness of glory:

> O Father!
> I will that those whom you have entrusted to me
> shall be at my side where I am:
> I want them to behold my glory,
> the glory you bestowed on me
> because you loved me
> before the world was founded. . . .
> dwell in them
> as I dwell in them myself (Jn 17:24, 26).

PRAYER

1. Jn 17:6-19   3. Jn 6:59-71   5. 1 Jn 4:1-6
2. Jn 17:20-26   4. Jn 10:11-21   6. Ac 4:32-37

25

". . . BUT ONE OF THE SOLDIERS PIERCED HIS SIDE WITH A LANCE AND IMMEDIATELY THERE CAME OUT BLOOD AND WATER" (Jn 19:34).

PAUL CLAUDEL, the French poet, in his *Hymn to the Sacred Heart*, states that in the *heart* of Jesus, pierced in death, a wound is torn open which plunges down to the *center* of the Trinity. John the Evangelist places Mary, the mother of Jesus, symbol of the Church, the New Eve, who begets us Christians into God's divine life, at the foot of the Cross.

Next to her on one side stands John the Beloved Disciple, symbol of all the loving members of the Church who contemplate the climax of God's mysterious and passionate love for each of us through the powerful symbol of Jesus' pierced heart and the emptying of its contents to the last drop of blood and water.

Mary Magdalene also stands there as a symbol of the repentant Christian who would fall passionately in love with Jesus crucified as he/she also experiences, in broken sinfulness, the burning love of the divine-human Savior.

Simone Weil dramatically writes that if God had not humiliated Himself for love of us, He would have been imperfect. St. Paul believes that God's power is manifested in our own weaknesses as it was in Jesus, the *Ebed Yahweh* or Suffering Servant. To the Corinthians Paul writes: "Why, there is more wisdom in the 'absurdity' of God than in all the 'wisdom' of men and more might in the 'weakness' of God than in all the might of men'' (1 Cor 1:25).

> But God chose what the world holds foolish, to put to shame the wise, and what the world holds weak God chose to put to shame the mighty, and what the world holds ignoble and despicable, and what counts for nought God chose, to bring to nought the things that count, lest any weak mortal should pride himself in God's sight. From him comes your union in Christ Jesus, who has become for us God-given wisdom and holiness and sanctification and redemption; so that, just as it is written, "Let him that takes pride, take pride in the Lord" (1 Cor 1:27-31).

IMAGE OF GOD'S EMPTYING LOVE

WE IN THE WESTERN WORLD STRIVE to find our identity in power and independence. We want absolute control so we suffer no ignorance and live in no mystery that exceeds our native human intelligence. The key to human success is measured by our being as completely independent as possible from others. We have not contemplated John's Wisdom in the person of Jesus emptied on the cross unto the last drop of blood and water. But we have preferred the wisdom of Nietzsche that whatever proceeds from power is good; whatever comes from weakness is bad.

We seek to prove that Jesus is truly God, of the same nature as the Heavenly Father, by His powerful miracles and healings. Yet we have forgotten His greatest revealing work in His "hour" when He would be lifted up on the cross as the Suffering Servant of God. God never looked more like Jesus and Jesus looked never more divine, of the same nature as the Father, than when He hung on the cross.

This is where John moves away from merely presenting Jesus in realistic, graphic details which stress, as in the Synoptic

Gospels, His suffering humanity, to give us an "imaging" by Jesus, the Divine Word made flesh, of the unseen God (Col 1:15) as *kenotic*, self-emptying love.

John's approach to the sufferings and death of Jesus always sees the last hours of His earthly existence in the light of a process of continued revelation that requires on the part of Christians, reading the details John presents, a truly contemplative, mystical spirit which moves far beyond the "objective" approach in the other Gospels. In these latter narratives Jesus is presented as the Expiator of our sins, the one who buys back our ransom from the forces of evil.

John appeals to the Holy Spirit, given in fullness only when Jesus dies. "He meant by this the Spirit whom those who believed in him were destined to receive. As yet there was no outpouring of the Spirit, because Jesus was not yet glorified" (Jn 7:39-40). For John the Christian cannot understand the revelation that Jesus is making on the cross in His "hour" except through the infusion by the Spirit of knowledge that surpasses all our human understanding. It is the experiential knowledge that St. Paul writes of: "With Christ I am nailed to the cross. It is now no longer I who live, but Christ lives in me. The life that I now live in this body, I live by faith in the Son of God, who loved me and sacrificed himself for me" (Gal 2:20-21).

Let us, therefore, stand at the foot of the cross and seek to enter through the pierced heart of Jesus crucified on Calvary into the very Trinitarian community of God. God is love, and true love is self-emptying for the other.

THE LOGIC OF LOVE

HAVE YOU SERIOUSLY AND OFTEN ASKED YOURSELF this question: "But why the cross? Why did Jesus *have* to die? Why did the Father decree that He die? It all seems so cruel, so gruesome!"

Surely the sufferings, His service on our behalf, which He
underwent in the Garden of Gethsemane and on Calvary,
cannot theologically be understood only by a legalistic atone-
ment theory. According to such thinking, God's justice de-
manded repayment by the suffering God-Man to atone for our
sinfulness. There must be more that the Word of God reveals to
us in deep contemplation of Christ's sufferings. This He does
through His Holy Spirit who unveils mysteries far beyond the
reach of our intellect.

Just as our human love knows various degrees of acting
out the love we have for another, so Jesus grew in His freedom
to surrender Himself completely to the Father. As Jesus experienced in prayerful communion His Heavenly Father's immense love for Him, especially at His baptism, the forty days
alone in the desert, His all-night vigils on the mountaintop,
during His public ministry, in Gethsemane and in those dying
moments on Calvary, He grew in His sensitivity to what love
was asking of Him by way of a self-gift back to the Father. Much
has been written about the psychological development of
Jesus' human consciousness. But because the Gospels are an
interpretation of the faith-experience of the early Christian
community concerning the person, Jesus Christ, we are always
left with the uncertainty of knowing, not only what words
attributed to Jesus were really His own, but above all of what
was his psychological state of consciousness at any stage of His
human development.

The Evangelist John gives us another approach as we
reflect on Jesus pierced on the cross out of love for us and the
Father. We can readily accept the fact that Jesus saw certain
actions decreed by the Father as clear commands, just as we
know clearly the commands of God in the ten commandments
that govern our basic relationships with God and neighbor.

Yet Jesus showed greater sensitivity to the Father's every
"wish." He strove to do whatever His conscience told Him

through the Spirit would be the Father's will. He sought to "please" the Father in all circumstances in His earthly life. Even in human love we can bring ourselves from time to time to forget ourselves and, in a burst of self-sacrifice for the one we love, we can "improvise" some gift that cost us a price in sacrifice to "flesh" out our love. This love is stirring within our hearts. We make a sacrifice, freely chosen, under no obligation through an expressed command or even a wish on the part of the one we love. Jesus, who progressively experienced in His humanity the love of the Father as no other person on the face of the earth had, sought to please His Father always. He wanted to make Him happy. So Jesus could say and live these words:

> . . . He whose ambassador I am is with me.
> He has not left me alone,
> because at all times I do
> what is pleasing to him (Jn 8:29-30).

CREATIVE SUFFERING

MUCH IN THE LIFE OF CHRIST, especially in His sufferings, passion and death, can be explained in His free choices to imitate and to reveal the outpouring love of total self-giving of the Father to His Son and through Him, His image, to each of us. I like to call it "creative suffering." It is what keeps love alive. It is fire touching dry wood and making it burst into flame too. Jesus, loved infinitely by the Father, was being driven in His human consciousness, not by any obligation, but by the consuming desire to take His life in His hands and in utter freedom to give it back to His beloved Father.

In a way we could say that Jesus, given who He was, the Word of the Father made flesh, "had" to pour Himself out or He would not have been what He was from all eternity, the perfect Word issuing from the Mind of God and returning in His complete "YES" in self-surrendering love to the Father. In emptying Himself by His own free choice to suffer more and more, Jesus was the revealing image of His Father. He was God's Word, God's presence in the world as infinite love going all the way, even unto death, speaking to us all of the Father.

The Suffering Servant now becomes better understood in His role of Revealer of God's love for us. There is light in the darkness of Jesus' *kenosis* or self-emptying. It is not merely that He *had* to suffer and die in order to save us from eternal death. Throughout His whole life Jesus freely chose, when there were possibilities, to descend into the heart of those who were lost, to descend into the suffering, dying heart of humanity. He freely wanted to become the poorest of the poor, the loneliest of all the abandoned in order that He might look like God. Who sees Him, sees the Father (Jn 14:9).

His love for His Father burned so strongly within Him that He chose to go into the dregs of humanity and to become one with the lowest of the lowly. He freely willed, by a human choice, to taste every ingredient in the bitter chalice that the world, in which the mystery of evil rules, could press to human lips.

LOVE UNTO DEATH

CAN WE NOT BELIEVE THAT JESUS, becoming the Suffering Servant of Yahweh, freely wanted to suffer and to be poured out like spilt wax in order that His human mind might be the perfect reflection of the Mind of God? His human consciousness was to become one with the consciousness of the Father. Jesus in His service to the world, entering into the very depths of sin and death and utter emptiness of self, was choosing humanly to be like God. It was His perfect way of imaging the eternal love of the Father for you and me. We have no other way of knowing the Father but through the Son. Here we have the perfect expression in human language of the very being of God. For this, John does not emphasize the realism of the sufferings of Christ. He chooses rather to highlight the awesome transcendence of the Trinity's love lifting us through such sufferings into the very heart of God and sharing with us a part of His glorious triune life.

Jesus had said: "The Father loves me because I lay down my life, and he wills that I should take it back again. No one can rob me of it. No, I lay it down of my own will. I have power to lay it down, and power to take it back again. Such is the charge I have received from my Father" (Jn 10:17-18). The Father loves Jesus because He lays down His life freely on our behalf. But this love burns so powerfully in the heart of Jesus because Jesus makes concrete in human terms our Father's love for us.

If the Father loves Jesus because Jesus makes explicit the Father's love for us, is it too farfetched that the Father also undergoes sufferings, seeing Jesus freely entering into the pit of darkness of human sinfulness and becoming a part of that? Can we not also accept the Father as a suffering servant on our behalf? It is true that the Father does not suffer physically since only Jesus is God-Man. But how can the Word suffer for us and the Mind which speaks that Word remain unmoved? Love cannot remain uninvolved in the sufferings of the one loved. The Father must be in His Word. The Word has meaning only because He is the exact Image of the Father who communicates Himself in His Word.

TO LIVE FOR OTHERS

As we enter through contemplative prayer into the "heart" of Jesus crucified and there experience divine love poured out for us unto the last drop of water and blood, the Spirit of the risen Jesus reveals to us, as "living waters" that flow out of the rock that is Christ (1 Cor 10:4), the depths of God's love for us. We can always confidently approach this sacred fountain, the rock that is Jesus, and be washed through the Spirit's revelation of God's love in the water and blood of Christ.

THE WOMB OF CHRIST'S SIDE

IT IS CERTAINLY the Holy Spirit who has revealed to mystics down through the ages as they contemplated the pierced heart of God on the cross, that from that side of Christ, the New Adam, we, the Church, the Spouse of Christ, the New Eve are brought to life. They had reflected prayerfully upon St. Paul's words:

> . . . just as Christ loved the Church, and delivered himself for her, that he might sanctify her by cleansing her in the bath of water with the accompanying word, in order to present to himself the Church in all her glory, devoid of blemish or wrinkle or anything of the kind, but that she may be holy and flawless (Ep 5:25-26).

More importantly they experienced daily, in prayer, what it means to enter into the "heart" of Christ, into the depths of His conscious love for each of us and there be reborn of His Spirit of love. A fitting close to this chapter which has led us from the great love of Jesus for us individually to His love for the Church is St. John Chrysostom's comment on the wounded side of Christ:

> The lance of the soldier opened the side of Christ, and behold . . . from his wounded side Christ built the Church, as once the first mother, Eve, was formed from Adam. Hence Paul says: Of his flesh we are and of his

bone. By that he means the wounded side of Jesus. As God took the rib out of Adam's side and from it formed the woman, so Christ gives us water and blood from his wounded side and forms from it the Church . . . there the slumber of Adam: here the death-sleep of Jesus.

The Church is formed out of the womb of Christ's heart which is the image of the heart or consciousness of the Father. Water and blood are the symbols of the life-giving power that Jesus, dying on the cross, gives to His Bride, the Church in the birth-giving waters of Baptism and the nourishing Body and Blood of Christ. Before such infinite love of God, made manifest in Christ Jesus, our response must be a similar return of emptying love by the power of Jesus' Spirit in us.

PRAYER

1. Jn 19:17-30
2. Jn 19:31-37
3. Jn 7:37-39
4. Ep 5:25-35
5. 1 Cor 10:1-5
6. Gn 2:18-25

26

"BLESSED ARE THOSE
WHO HAVE NOT SEEN AND YET BELIEVE"
(Jn 20:29)

THE BYZANTINE ICON of the resurrection is never an objectivized picture of the historical Jesus coming out of the tomb, as if He had died and three days later was resuscitated, returning to his "normal" human existence on this earth. Rather, Jesus is depicted as pulling an aged man out of the bowels of the earth. It is an artistic commentary on the Christian theological truth that Jesus, by His resurrection, entered into the hellish areas of human existence and there destroyed death and sin. Usually this icon portrays Christ stepping over the doors of hell with the instruments of His passion scattered about. He pulls Adam out of the underworld, while Hades is personified as a demon trying to hold him back.

Eastern Christianity is highly influenced by the Gospel of John. Resurrection according to John is a new age as God *now* is restoring the human race to a new life in Christ. A new creation, not only of the risen Jesus, but of human beings sharing in His new life and the whole cosmos transfigured by His glorious presence, has begun. John pictures Jesus, the crucified one, as having been raised from the dead; as being preached by His followers as the Son of God, the Lord (*Kyrios*) and Redeemer; and as God's saving act. He is a power, present and operative in the Christian community through the Spirit whom the risen Lord pours out upon His united followers.

Jesus acts out on the Johannine pages the words John writes in the Book of Revelation: "Do not be afraid. I am the First and the Last and the Living One. I was dead, but how wonderful, I live for ever and ever, and have the keys of death and of the nether world" (Rv 1:17-18). Jesus "died and was raised to life" (2 Cor 5:15) for us that we might have eternal life.

John's Gospel is a call to see Jesus Christ, from the first page of his Prologue to the end of the Gospel, from the perspective of His glorious, resurrectional presence within the Christian community. Its readers are called to enter into the highest level of encountering the risen Jesus and through Him and His Spirit to live in faith, hope and love in the basic community of all communities of love, the Trinity. John calls us to go beyond any mere sense knowledge that could never touch the reality of Jesus' resurrection which lies outside of such certain empirical understanding. Those are called "blessed" who have not "seen" this even with their human intellection, but have become the recipients of the gift from the Spirit of the risen Jesus to "believe."

As the Christian learns to let go of his/her control over the reality of the historical Jesus, Jesus is experienced as near and ready to bring new power and eternal life to the believer.

THE RISEN LORD
AS EXPERIENCED BY THE COMMUNITY

THERE ARE GIVEN IN THE NEW TESTAMENT three types of testimonies to the resurrection of Christ. There are the *confessional formulas*, as for example, the one found in 1 Corinthians 5:3-5. There are *hymns* that predominantly came out of the Liturgy celebrated by the communities of believers where in the Eucharist they profoundly opened themselves up to the actions of Jesus as risen and all-powerful through the release of His Spirit. And, lastly, there are the *Easter stories* of Jesus' appearances to various individuals or groups of His disciples.

It is mainly the latter genre that John chose to lead Christians into the transfiguring presence and power of the risen Lord. He shapes the stories of the appearances of Jesus to His followers to fit his own theology of Easter. Thus we have some bits of historical traditions, but, more basically, we are presented with important theological narratives in dramatic form.

John's teachings about the resurrection of Jesus say something, not only about Jesus, but about God as well. The ultimate issue behind all the resurrectional narratives in John's Gospel is our understanding of God, through Jesus risen, who is now empowered by the Father to whom He has "returned," becoming for the Christian community the Way, the Truth and the Life that brings believers into eternal life, even now. The disciples who saw Jesus in apparitions had to risk "believing" beyond any sense certitude they may have had through the apparitions. In the same way, Christians who had not seen Him in apparitions had to approach the mystery of Jesus — risen and present in this world now in a new way of existing that can only be known through the Holy Spirit — through a risk, the "risk" of faith.

The Good News presented on the pages of John's Gospel is that this same historical Jesus of Nazareth lives! He is actively involved as the Son of God in the present life, thought and behavior of the community. He invites us to share with Him the very Trinitarian life of the Godhead. In the power of Jesus' *passover* from death to new life, we can now receive the Spirit of His love and enter into a new existence that destroys the limitations imposed upon our historical time and space by sin, death and the "elements of the world." We belong to Christ, the Victor, as the branches belong and abide in the Vine, since He has conquered all sin and death. In the experience of sharing, even now, in Christ's victory as we die to our selfishness and rise by the Spirit of love to love for others, we can bring forth abundant fruit. We can "love one another" (Jn 15:17) as Jesus and the Father love us.

A NEW TIME AND A NEW SPACE

THE POET W.H. Auden well describes space and time in terms of meaningful, loving relationships which come close to John's concept of space and time as applied to Jesus' resurrection and His new living relationships to us still on this earth.

Space is the Whom our loves are needed by
Time is our choice of How to love and Why.

According to Johannine theology, Jesus risen now lives in a
new time. It is the *kairos* or salvific time in which we can
choose to enter into His victory over sin and death through our
belief and commitment to His abiding presence within us
individually and within the Christian community and be
healed of our death-dealing isolation and self-centeredness.
We can meet Jesus risen only by entering into His new time and
His new space. The apparitions for John are not the essential
basis for belief in Jesus. John uses these to lead us into the
theology of belief in the resurrection which cannot depend on
any sense or historical knowledge of events rooted in the "old
time," the *chronos* that limits belief in God and all too often
holds us in isolation and in death-dealing independence from
others. Men and women in John's Gospel witness to their
encounter with the risen Jesus by faith, not because they understood empirically. John shows us that this is the basis for the
faith of the "beloved disciple" who believed, not because of an
apparition of his Lord, but only through the gift of faith, beyond
all reasoning and sense experiences. His faith is in contrast to
Thomas' lack of faith and willingness to believe only through
touching Jesus.

Jesus risen is able to send His disciples the vivifying Spirit,
who alone could lead them into the *now* experience of Jesus
raising them beyond sin and death into a share of His resurrection and eternal life. The resurrection of Christ is a new beginning which brings to an end the domination of historical time
and space, even though His presence and active, involving
power happen within the orbit of earthly time and space. God
has now entered mysteriously into the history of humanity and
from within is setting about to destroy sin, corruption and
death. This is done fully in Jesus. But God acts gradually

through Jesus' risen presence living in His members, who become His leaven, to raise all of humanity into a sharing of the same new life of Christ.

Jesus risen now meets His disciples in a new space. That space lies within the individual Christian in what Scripture calls the "heart." It is there in the Spirit of faith, hope and love that Christians are to experience their true selves as being "in Christ Jesus." Eternal life is received in the spaceless space of Christ's healing love. In the consciousness that the Spirit of the risen Lord brings the Christian, he/she becomes baptized by the Spirit into a greater oneness with Him. Eternal life is especially experienced in the sacraments, as Christians eat the Bread of Life and drink His blood. Jesus' risen presence is also present in His Word as it is preached within the Body, the Church. He becomes present in the teaching and guidance of the Church through its authority with its charism to build up the Body in truth and love. He is present as risen when we serve one another in love. Every member is able to be the "space" in which the risen Jesus operates by seeking to "wash" the feet of others, as Jesus did.

AN INDWELLING PRESENCE

OVER AND OVER in the pages of the New Testament we find paradoxes and antitheses that seek by various metaphors or symbols to express the mystery of God's in-breaking love in order to share with us His very own Trinitarian life. We see this especially present in the pages of the Johannine Gospel. Jesus preached about death-life, darkness-light, bondage-freedom. But, above all, He came among us and lived these paradoxes. He was the light that came into the darkness, even though the darkness did not comprehend Him (Jn 1:9-11). He came to bring life, and that more abundantly, to those who were sick and dying (10:10). He was the power in whom all things were created and made (1:2); yet He appeared in weakness, crucified and emptied out on the cross for love of us. In His humiliations He was lifted up (12:32) and exalted in glory by His Father.

His defeat on the cross by the powers of evil led to eternal victory over sin and death. His shame turned to glory. And He holds out to us the same possibility of suffering with Him in order that we might also enter into glory with Him. He has destroyed sin and death and has allowed us to be "reborn" from above by His Spirit (Jn 3:3, 5). We have been baptized into His death, and He has raised us to new life. He has gone away from this earth for a short while and yet He will return and now remains always with us, as He and the Father come and abide within us to share their Trinitarian life with us (14:23).

LIVING IN THE VICTORY OF THE LORD

TO LIVE IN THE MYSTERY of Jesus' resurrection is to allow His victory to exercise daily a transforming power in our lives. John uses the title, Lord (*Kyrios* in Greek) fourteen times in presenting the risen Jesus. We see a peculiar shifting back and forth between the intimacy that Jesus enjoyed with His "friends" before His death and yet a distance of awesome transcendence. The risen Jesus is no longer part of this world. He has taken His abode in the divine sphere, by "returning to the Father." Yet the good news is that Jesus in a more intimate manner now lives within the community of love and within the individual disciple who believes that Jesus is the Son of God, to whom has been given all power on earth and in heaven.

Christ by His resurrection has conquered the limitations imposed upon time and space by our sinful condition and, through the release of His Spirit within our hearts, we are able to live on a new level of consciousness that explodes time and space into an exciting, ever *now* moment, the *kairos* time of salvation. In this new time, the risen and exalted Jesus sweeps us into a sharing in His power and glory that knows none of the limitations of ordinary time and space.

A COMMITMENT OF LOVE

DEATH AND SIN are being destroyed as we experience in the "sacrament of the present moment" the burning love of God almighty, three Persons in a oneness of love for us as individuals and as members of the total Christ. It is this experienced love of God made manifest to us daily through the Spirit of the risen Jesus that conquers all death-dealing elements in our lives and in our world and leads us into a new oneness with Him. Then in such new life nothing really matters, or, rather, everything matters in a new and exciting way. "You, little children, are born of God, and you have overcome the false teachers, because God who is in you is greater than the devil who is in the world" (1 Jn 4:4).

Christianity calls out a response in love to the ever-present love of God as Trinity, a community of love. It is the love of God in the personalized relationships of Father, Son and Holy Spirit, dwelling within us individually and within the Body of Christ, the Church, that is experienced as we die to the distortion of our own reason as the ultimate criterion of true wisdom and open ourselves to the wisdom of Christ crucified, risen and exalted in glory.

A *NOW* ETERNITY

FOR JOHN, eternity is not what begins when our historical time ceases. It is the everlasting time and life of God; it is already the new time in which we Christians now live in the Trinity. This "new time" of salvation cuts down vertically through our broken, horizontal time that is riddled by what Scripture calls "sin and death." This new time of Christ intersects the old, broken time and becomes a transforming leaven changing historical time into salvific time. This doesn't mean that the old time is destroyed but rather that it is transformed from within. It is a gradual consummation of time through the presence of the risen Lord inserted into the alienated materiality of the universe.

Such a process, begun in embryonic form in our Baptism, is like a seed that already contains the fruit. Still it necessitates a steady growth with each moment's victory a preparation for the next conquest, "from glory to glory." "Jesus is already risen" is the shout we raise up, as the early Christians did. He has gone from the world in the sense that now only by faith can He be experienced and be "seen." John presents us this essential teaching in the apparitions of Jesus risen to Mary Magdalene (Jn 20:1-18), to the disciples riddled by fear as they hid behind bolted doors (20:19-23), then to Thomas with the other disciples (20:24-31), and in the final recorded apparition of Jesus to His disciples on the shore of Lake Tiberias (21:1-23).

And He will come again in the fullness of glory. But the Good News John presents to us through the apparitions of the risen Jesus — news that gives us the courage to live dynamically this present moment with all of its "groaning in travail" (Rm 8:22) — is that this risen Jesus is still with us! He is now releasing His loving Spirit who fills us with love and takes away our fears so that we can enter into the process of becoming living members of the risen Body of Christ, the Lord. It is only the Spirit who can reveal to us in any given moment the presence of Christ as risen. This glorified Christ is actually one with us in His power and transforming glory. No fear can be with us for His loving presence and power drive out all fear (1 Jn 4:8).

The Spirit is seen at work in Christ's resurrection as the Fulfiller of the original purpose of God's creation. The Spirit makes it possible for us to experience the presence and transforming power of the *Kyrios*, the risen Christ, to whom all power in heaven and on earth has been given.

OUR RESPONSE

OUR RESPONSE not only determines the degree of how fully actualized we will become as human beings, but it influences how fully risen the entire Christ will become in the final glorification of "God in all." Our lives are to be apostolic. We have been commissioned and sent by Christ to bring forth the fruit of love by building up a loving community: the Body of Christ, the Church (Jn 15:6). To bear the fruit of love is to remain in Christ. To be united with Jesus risen is the same as dying to selfishness. Positively, being united with Christ means putting on the new person that we have become by living in the power of His resurrection.

The grain of wheat must be ground and the grapes pressed to make the flour and the wine which will be transformed into the Body and Blood of Christ as the fulfillment of His resurrectional life captured in the Eucharist. So we too must also die to whatever is false in our being or against our true nature. We must be pressed by Divine Love until there is nothing of self left so that we live now no longer as ourselves, but Christ Jesus lives in us (Gal 2:20). It is only through such a death unto new life that Christ will be able to live within us and we will be able to go forth to bring about that abundant fruit that Christ has destined to be produced through our humble instrumentality in bringing Him to many others. Through our ordinary work done in love by putting on Christ's mind, abiding in His word, we can bring the resurrectional transformation to the materiality of this universe in which we form a very small, but important, element.

The early disciples, as shown in John's Gospel, were very much aware, not only that the historical Jesus was alive and present more powerfully to them than before in His historical existence, but also that they themselves were being called to witness all over the world to this reality of the presence and the power of the Trinity, Father, Son and Holy Spirit, as immanently present through the Christians and thus present through them to this broken world. They were building up the Body of Christ, until the second coming of the Lord.

Christ is risen, but remains hidden within the Church and the world that is a part of the Church. The Church looks forward longingly and by active involvement in surrendering love and service to Jesus to build His total Body. Then there will be a corporate resurrection when others not of Jesus' fold will be brought into one fold and under one Shepherd (Jn 10:16-17). Through the cooperation of Christians the Cosmic Christ is moving this world to its completion. The universe will not be annihilated, but will be transformed into a sharing of the resurrectional life of Christ. A most fitting close to our meditations on the risen Jesus and the new creation that began with the first words of John's Prologue: "All things came into being through him, and without him there came to be not one thing that has come to be . . ." (Jn 1:3) is John's final vision of Heaven: the fulfillment of God's creation of all things in His Word.

How wonderful! God's dwelling place is among men;
   he shall make his home among them.
They shall be his people,
   and God himself shall abide in their midst.
He shall wipe away every tear from their eyes.
   No longer will there be death.
No longer will there be mourning
   or cry of anguish or pain.
Because the former things have passed.

He who was seated on the throne said,
"See, I make all things new."
Then he added, "Write, because these words are
   trustworthy and true."
He said to me,
   "It is done. I am the Alpha and the Omega,
   the beginning and the end.
To him who thirsts I will give of the water of life
   free of charge from the fountain.
He who is victorious shall possess these blessings,
   and I will be his God, and he shall be my son" (Rv 21:3-7).

PRAYER

1. Jn 20:1-18
2. Jn 20:19-23
3. Jn 20:24-31
4. Jn 21:1-14
5. Jn 21:15-25
6. Rv 1:17-20; 21:3-7